A Passion for Survival

The True Story of Marie Anne and Louis Payzant in Eighteenth-century Nova Scotia

Linda G. Layton

NIMBUS
PUBLISHING

Nimbus Publishing Limited
PO Box 9166, Halifax, NS, B3K 5M8
(902) 455-4286

Printed and bound in Canada
Design: JWD Communications Ltd
Cover image: Sixty years before John Elliott Woolford painted this "View on the road from Windsor...1817," Marie Anne and her four children passed through the area with their Maliseet captors, en route to Quebec city. (courtesy Nova Scotia Museum)

National Library of Canada Cataloguing in Publication

Layton, Linda G.
A passion for survival : the true story of Marie Anne
and Louis Payzant in eighteenth-century Nova Scotia /
Linda G. Layton.
Includes bibliographical references.
ISBN 1-55109-457-6

1. Payzant, Marie Anne, ca. 1711-1796. 2. Payzant, Louis, ca. 1695-1756. 3. Nova Scotia—History—1713-1775—Biography. 4. Canada—History—Seven Years' War, 1755-1763—Prisoners and prisons. 5. Canada—History--1713-1763 (New France)—Biography. 6. Huguenots—Canada--Biography. I. Title.

FC384.1.P39L39 2003   971.01'88'0922   C2003-903217-5
F1030.P29L39 2003

Canada   The Canada Council | Le Conseil des Arts
          for the Arts | du Canada

We acknowledge the financial support of the Government of Canada through the Book Publishing Industry Development Program (BPIDP) and the Canada Council for our publishing activities.

Contents

Preface vii

A Preview xv

Chapter 1 – Louis in Caen (ca. 1695–1739) 1

Chapter 2 – Jersey, Island of Refuge (1739-1753) 22

Chapter 3 – Lunenburg, a New Beginning (1753-1756) 38

Chapter 4 – Island Attack (1756) 49

Chapter 5 – Maliseet Trek (1756) 58

Chapter 6 – Quebec Captivity (1756-1760) 67

Chapter 7 – Falmouth, Another Beginning (1761-1796) 84

Epilogue 95

Endnotes 120

Image Sources 134

Bibliography 135

Tintype of Nellie Gertrude Harlow on her mother Lavinia's lap, Liverpool, Nova Scotia, ca. 1884. It was this photograph of the author's maternal grandmother that inspired her to explore the family history.

Preface

THROUGH THE TINTYPE

I was fourteen when my maternal grandmother, "Nana," died in Toronto in 1961. She was visiting her two older sisters when one of them, Aunt Gussie, found her on the floor beside her bed, dead from a heart attack. Aunt Gussie was the same sister who raised Nana from the age of twelve after their mother died in 1895 in Liverpool, Nova Scotia.

I was very close to Nana (Nellie Gertrude Payzant, née Harlow, 1883–1961) because she lived with my parents, sister, and me in Edmonton, Alberta, during four of her fifteen years of widowhood. After her funeral in Toronto, her remains were cremated and burial was planned for the plot beside her husband in Nova Scotia. We flew to Toronto to visit with family. While we were there, Aunt Gussie told me a few stories about growing up in Liverpool, and passed on to me a tintype photograph dating from 1884. I was absolutely fascinated. It showed Nana as an infant on her mother's lap, wearing a little dress that Aunt Gussie had made. I wanted to climb right into the photo and look around at their environment—was everything really in black and white with the only colour being the pink on everyone's cheeks? What was going on in the world at that time? A fountain of questions bubbled up as I stared at every detail. This simple tintype photograph captured my imagination and drew me into years of exploration of my family history.

That summer of 1961, I had the privilege of carrying the urn containing Nana's ashes on my lap as we flew to Nova Scotia for the burial. I found Nova Scotia so different from Edmonton. My hometown, named capital of the new province of Alberta in 1905, is so new in comparison. (Just south of Edmonton, "my" oil derrick, Alberta's first successful oil well, still stands tall. For twenty-eight years they searched for oil, and on February 13, 1947, the day I was born, the well "blew in,"spewing oil and gas, and ushering in the economic boom of the 1950s.) Other than the deep valley of the North Saskatchewan River, the land is flat, and the blue sky endless. Nova Scotia's landscape is more wooded and hilly, with gentle valleys, and rugged coasts along the Bay of Fundy and the Atlantic Ocean.

Towns in Nova Scotia are different too—no straight roads with avenues running east and west and streets north and south. In Nova Scotia the streets follow the natural contours of the land, as they were laid many generations ago.

The house my mother grew up in was built in 1854. Her father, Alfred Doull Payzant (always known as "A.D."), had bought it in 1896 for $1,600 when, at age twenty-eight, he was a dashing bachelor and already a successful businessman. I loved the sense of history in the town of Canning in the Annapolis Valley and the fact that I was related to so many people in the area (my dad was born in nearby Kentville). I wanted to know more.

It was then that I learned the story of my French ancestor Marie Anne Payzant (circa 1711–1796) and her husband Louis Payzant (circa 1695–1756), who had emigrated to Nova Scotia. Studying eighteenth-century Canadian history took on new meaning for me because my ancestors were there—living, breathing, laughing, and crying. They were more than just names and dates on a page.

I developed an interest in my genealogy and discovered I had deep roots in Nova Scotia: all four of my grandparents were born there. My French ancestors (Payzants) landed in Halifax, then Lunenburg in 1753. My American ancestors (Harlows), descended from *Mayflower* Puritans, moved north in 1760. My Yorkshire ancestors (Laytons) arrived in 1774 in Falmouth, and my Scottish ancestors (MacLeods) landed in Cape Breton in 1806.

I'm fortunate that genealogical books have been written on all four families. The most exciting story, however, is about the Payzant family. In 1970, when Marion M. Payzant published her long-awaited book on the Payzants, I devoured the pages on the family history.[1] However, I found the information confusing—the jumble of facts begged to be organized into a chronological story.

In 1985 a friend sent me a 1974 magazine he had stumbled across that contained a fictional account of Marie Anne and Louis Payzant.[2] After reading the story, I realized it was based on previous ones that

A.D. and Nellie Payzant at home, now 9711 Main Street, Canning, Nova Scotia, 1910.

contained errors. I resolved right then to take on the task of writing a simplified and accurate historical version that would highlight the story of these Canadian pioneers.

The quest became an obsession. Over the years I collected as many versions of the story as I could. I researched the historical period, discovered

Notes on Louis Payzant written by A.D. Payzant in Canning, Nova Scotia, ca. 1896.

new information, and dug up documents, some of which bore Marie Anne's and Louis' signatures. What a thrill to find those!

In 1989 I inherited a document that had been given to my great-grandfather William Henry Payzant (1827–1885) in the 1870s.[3] Written in 1756, it refers to Louis Payzant after he had settled in Nova Scotia. As much as I valued owning it, I felt the document should be shared with other researchers and descendants. In 1995 I donated it to the Public Archives of Nova Scotia (now Nova Scotia Archives and Records Management).[4]

While reading original 1890s notes and correspondence by my grandfather, A.D. Payzant, I realized that I share with him the same burning desire to know the whole story. I know he'd be so pleased to read this book, and delighted to learn more about his ancestors' lives prior to their arrival in Nova Scotia.

It's interesting to note the similarities between A.D. Payzant (who died in 1945, two years before I was born) and his great-great grandfather Louis Payzant (circa 1695–1756). They were dry goods merchants who each took over their family business when their fathers died. My grandfather was fifteen years older than his bride; Louis was sixteen years older than Marie Anne. I inherited a cedar box of buttons from my grandfather's store; in 1739 Louis had in his inventory ninety-six dozen buttons.

My grandfather's, and others', fascination with the Payzant family history is evident in my mother's account of a day in the early 1930s:

> One of my childhood memories is of Dad at home in Canning, N.S., welcoming a namesake from Falmouth, N.S. This gentleman had driven all the way by horse and buggy to show Dad his material regarding Marie Payzant.
>
> I went off to tend the store in Dad's absence, Mother playing the piano, and the horse and buggy tied up in the church barn next door.
>
> After many, many years I can still see those two gentlemen side by side in the glassed-in veranda hunched over the material, absorbed in the past."[5]

NAMING

Choosing the right name for Marie Anne in this book took some consideration. In eighteenth-century France, "Marie" was the most popular woman's name as a single name and in combination names. It was often placed first and being so common, was sometimes disregarded. This is likely why she is referred to as "Anne Noget" in original French documents. There is no way to verify this, however, since Huguenot church records for her town in 1711 (the year of her baptism) have been destroyed. In Nova Scotia in 1755, she was "Anna Paysant," as written by a German. Once she returned again to Nova Scotia in 1760, however, she was "Mary Payzant" or "Mary Ann Caigin" (after her 1762 remarriage).

Yes, she really is the same person: "Louis Paisant and Miss Anne Noget"[6] were married in Jersey in 1740. Also, "Mary Paysant" was the confirmed owner of "Paysants Island" in Mahone Bay in 1761.[7] She's usually referred to as "Mary Payzant" in documents and stories from the 1760s to 1921, in which historian Archibald MacMechan referred to her as "Marie Payzant"—the name used ever since.[8] However, in her 1970 book, family genealogist Marion M. Payzant refers to her as: "Anne Noget," "Marie Anne Noget," "Mary Anne Nazette," "Marie Ann Noguet," "Mary Anne (Noget) Payzant," "Mary Payzant," and "Marie Payzant." B.C. Cuthbertson, in his entry on John Payzant in the *Dictionary of Canadian Biography*, notes that John's mother was "Marie-Anne Noguet (Nazette)."[9] For the sake of consistency, I refer to her as "Marie Anne Noget" before her first marriage, and "Marie Anne Payzant" afterwards.

Her signature below was written in Quebec in December 1756:

The spelling of Louis Payzant's surname changed several times, from Paisant to Paysant to Payzant. The Middle French word *paisant* originates from the Old French *pais* ("country" or "inhabitant of a district"), from the Latin *pagus* (district). The English word "peasant," from the same origin, has been used since the fifteenth century.[11]

In France people began to use surnames around 1000 AD. Later, the upper classes passed on family names to their offspring. Most early names were based on place of residence or occupation—"country dweller" in the case of Payzant. Marion Payzant states that the origin of "Paisant" is "a compatriot, a fellow citizen, a lover of one's country."[12]

In the seventeenth and eighteenth centuries, Paisants were among the French Huguenots (Protestants) who escaped religious persecution and fled to England. Some of them supposedly anglicized their surname to "Pheasant." That's likely why the British coat of arms for "Payzant," as described in Burke's *General Armory of England, Scotland, Ireland, and Wales*, depicts a pheasant.[13]

Spelling was inconsistent in the eighteenth century. The letters "i" and "y" were often interchanged. Even though almost all references to the "Paisant" family were spelled as such in France, Louis signed his name with a "y." There is no difference in the French pronunciation of "s" and "z" in the middle of names such as Paysant and Payzant. Louis chose to use mostly the "s."

Variations on the spelling of "Payzant" by eighteenth-century clerks in Nova Scotia and Quebec all indicate a similar pronunciation:

Pizant, Pézant, Phisant, Peaysant, and even Baissang! The English pronunciation of "Payzant" can vary, but the more common way in Nova Scotia "stresses the last syllable to rhyme with "they cawn't."[14] Phonetically, it's "puh-zawnt," or "puh-zant."

With his quill pen, Louis signed his name in both a formal and informal signature:

15

16

In his informal signature, the two dots over the "u" indicate that it is "u" and not "v," which in the sixteenth and seventeenth centuries were both written as "v."[17] (The third dot is over the "i.")

Louis and Marie Anne's children, born in Jersey, Channel Islands, were given French names: Philippe, Marie, Jean, and Louis. When they immigrated to Nova Scotia, however, the names were anglicized to Philip, Mary, John, and Lewis, which I use in this book.

SOURCES

I have relied on primary documents for the facts of the Payzant story, since the diverse accounts in my collection vary in their details. Early secondary documents have credibility; most of the later ones don't.

French documents used in the Caen trial of Louis Payzant provide fascinating details of his life from 1738 to 1741.[18] Church records in St. Helier, Jersey, document the marriage, baptisms, and burials of family members from 1740 to 1751.[19]

Three items from 1756 are invaluable. Just three days after the raid on Payzant's Island, twenty-six-year old Dettlieb Christopher Jessen, deputy provost marshal of Lunenburg, Nova Scotia, recorded the gruesome details.[20] Marie Anne's abjuration in Quebec reveals her age and origin[21]; the baptism of Lisette Payzant lists her original name (Louise Catherine), and notes that her godfather was a merchant like her father.[22]

In 1810, when John Payzant (second son of Marie Anne and Louis) was sixty-one and a minister in Liverpool, Nova Scotia, he wrote a memoir on his ministry, in which he devoted only a few pages to his origin, the devastating event, and his subsequent confusion as a youth.[23] Shortly before Lewis Payzant (third son of Marie Anne and Louis) died in 1845 at the age of ninety-four, he gave an interview to Reverend Silas T. Rand, which was published seven years later.[24] Lewis' eldest son recalled many details of his father's life, which were recorded in 1860 by his thirty-year-old grandson, Dr. Elias N. Payzant, a dentist in Hantsport, Nova Scotia.[25] If the other three children of Marie Anne and Louis left memoirs of their lives, I am unaware of their existence.

The True Story of Marie Anne and Louis Payzant: A Preview

I picture my fourth great-grandmother as a carefree nine year old in 1720, running up one of the rolling green hills surrounding her village of Condé-sur-Noireau in Normandy, France. The wind billows her long dark purple dress and tosses her long hair—her mother will not be pleased to know she's taken off her clean white cap. Marie Anne Noget pauses halfway up, looks down, and admires the sun-dappled cluster of houses around the seigneur's château.

That same year, thirty-three kilometres northeast in the city of Caen, her future husband, a twenty-five-year-old merchant, purposefully strides along the bustling, cobblestoned rue Saint Pierre to meet a business colleague. He is well-dressed and draws admiring glances, as well he should—he and his parents sell shoes, hose, fabric, and tailoring and dressmaking supplies. Trying to side-step the occasional puddle to save his buckled black shoes, he doesn't make it: his white knee-high stockings are splashed. He should have worn gaiters. The lace under his wide cuff shows as

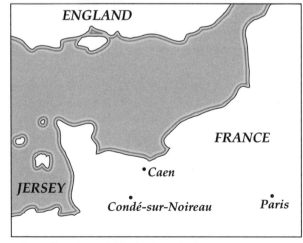

Map of Louis and Marie Anne's France.

he waves to a friend. A sudden gust shifts his white wig slightly and flips the lace jabot up to his chin. He's pleased with his new dark blue silk breeches and long vest. A row of brass buttons runs the length of his brocade jacket down to the knees. Louis Payzant glances up to admire the carvings of saints on the front of a merchant's house as he passes, but he doesn't believe in them—he's a Huguenot.

Both Marie Anne and Louis are bourgeois Huguenots: the sunny days of their youth are overcast by persecution at the hands of the Roman Catholic king and his government. Forced to flee France in search of freedom, they eventually take the adventurous leap to the New World in search of prosperity. Unfortunately the winds of war between France and Britain envelop them. The resulting tragedy almost obliterates the original North American Payzants.

Marie Anne may reflect on her memory of that carefree morning romp on the hills to comfort her later in life, as she struggles through a maelstrom of emotions—stark fear, grief, despondency, hatred, dread, loneliness, and resentment—before eventually finding peace.

CHAPTER ONE

Louis in Caen
(ca. 1695–1739)

Lefebvre, a sixty-year-old farmer, took great delight in his beloved child Magdalen—the apple of his eye. He, his invalid wife, Marie, and their grown sons and their families ran the ancestral farm, selling corn and fruit from their orchards. The sons spun wool from their sheep on cold winter evenings. Their wives spun flax from the farm into linen for the little girl's trousseau. They were completely self-sufficient.

In the fall of 1685, Lefebvre rode his horse to the cattle fair at Avranches, on the west coast of Normandy, France, to buy a cow for fattening over the winter. There, he learned from his fellow Huguenots about the new legislation that aimed to eliminate their Protestant religion from the country. They recited a long list of drastic measures. The most fearsome to Lefebvre was the stipulation that all Huguenot children seven years of age and under be taken from their parents to be educated by Roman Catholic monks or nuns. He couldn't imagine living without his precious Magdalen! Forgetting the cow, he spurred his horse homeward, tears blurring his vision.

He dashed into the house and covered his little girl with kisses. After telling his wife the news, they decided to send Magdalen out of the country so she could be free. Neighbours passing by on their way to Avranches had just told Marie of a fishing boat—due to leave that night from a nearby port—that would be taking local apples and pears to Jersey, where the orchard crops had failed. The captain was a trusted family friend.

"God will take care of our precious child," Marie cried to her husband, "and keep her safe from harm, til we two—or you, at least, dear

1

husband—can leave this accursed land. Or, if we cannot follow her, she will be safe for heaven; whereas, if she stays here to be taken to the terrible convent, hell will be her portion, and we shall never see her again—never!"

Hitching his cart to a fresh horse, Lefebvre filled it with a straw mattress and there tenderly placed his daughter, concealed in sackcloth in case they met Roman Catholic spies. Marie quickly filled a chest with clothes and a few trousseau items and her husband tucked it in beside Magdalen. Father and daughter headed north to Granville. He coaxed her to eat the food prepared by her mother, and, occasionally, with labour-hardened fingers, he stroked her cheeks and smoothed her hair. They arrived at the quay without incident. He handed his precious bundle over to the captain, who smuggled her on board past the inspectors.

Lefebvre returned home with such a heavy heart that he took to his bed, fell ill and died, soon followed by his wife. Magdalen was well cared for and eventually moved to London to live with two maiden aunts. Her descendants have passed down her story from generation to generation.[1]

Such was the situation in France when Louis Payzant, progenitor of the Payzant family in North America, was born circa 1695. Roman Catholic King Louis XIV, fearing the growing power of the middle-class Huguenots, was pressuring them to renounce their Protestantism, causing many to flee the country. Despite this oppression, Louis Payzant, a Huguenot in the predominantly Protestant city of Caen, in the province of Normandy, became a merchant like his parents.

His Norman genes may have included some Viking blood, contributing to the entrepreneurial spirit he displayed as a successful merchant. His Norse bloodline may also have provided the impetus for a remarkable adventure he began in middle age, when most men of Louis' era would have been content to spend the day sitting in front of the fireplace smoking a pipe.

In 911, the Vikings and their chieftain Rollo sailed south, invading the coasts of Gaul (France), which included the former hamlet known by the Romans in the first century AD as Cadomus, later Caen. Rollo claimed the whole area as the duchy of Normandy, named after these Scandinavian pirates, also known as Northmen, Norsemen, or Normans. They assimilated into the Frankish culture, adopted Christianity, and quickly developed the duchy into a powerful medieval state.

In the eleventh century, Duke William of Normandy built a château on a rocky spur in Caen, his favourite city, overlooking the confluence of the Odon (named after William's brother) and Orne rivers, 14 kilometres south of the English Channel and 223 kilometres northwest of Paris. In 1066 William expanded his domain across the English Channel. While king of England, he died in his capital city of Rouen, France, in 1087. He was not buried there, however, nor in England, but in Caen, in the Abbaye aux Hommes (men's abbey). Four years earlier, his wife Matilda of Flanders had also been buried in Caen in the Abbaye aux Dames (women's abbey). William and Matilda had built the abbeys to placate the pope, who objected to their marriage because they were fifth cousins (Rollo being their common ancestor).

Caen was one of the first centres of the Huguenot faith in France. The Huguenots thought of themselves as reformers, resisting conformity and submission to the political domination of the Roman Catholic Church. They were influenced by the writings of German monk Martin Luther and French theologian John Calvin.

Calvin, a priest and lawyer, published his *Institutes of the Christian Religion* in 1536 after experiencing a sudden conversion at the age of twenty-four. He moved to Geneva, Switzerland, and established a model Christian community based on Biblical principles by assimilating the church into the city government. Other reformers flocked to study the model community in Geneva, where Calvinists comprised more than one third of the population. Calvin put an end to monasteries and celibacy, and designed a moral code for Genevan citizens.

The French government called this dissenting church the "RPR" (Religion Prétendue Réformée, or the Alleged Reformed Religion), and regarded its adherents as heretics who had deviated from the one true religion. Because of this view, the Huguenot persecution lasted for over two centuries: from the rise of the Protestant movement in the 1550s (the Reformation) to the French Revolution in 1789.

According to Calvinist doctrine, those who led a saintly life could be saved, communion was symbolic, the church should not be subordinate to the state, and presbyteries (elected bodies of ministers and laymen) should govern the church. Hard, honest work, industry, and thrift were forms of moral virtue that led to business success, which in turn, was evidence of God's grace. These views helped create a pro-commerce climate that made the bourgeoisie (middle class) an eager group to adopt Calvinism.

Calvin sent missionaries to spread the new faith among the nobles, bourgeoisie, and artisans; by 1560 France's two thousand Huguenot communities included half the country's nobility and a third of its middle class. Those who embraced Calvinism were more than the

Sixteenth-century houses with carved half-timbering, rue Saint Pierre, Caen, France, 2001.

Huguenots in France—they included Puritans in England (and later America), Presbyterians in Scotland, and eventually, Congregationalists in America. As Calvinism acquired a firm hold in France, the Crown became increasingly concerned about rebellious Huguenot nobles (primarily in southwest France). That's why King Henry II, in the 1550s, began the persecution of Huguenots in earnest by burning them at the stake.[2]

Twenty years later the harassment escalated. In 1572 in Paris, the Protestant leader Henry of Navarre married Catherine de Medici, the daughter of the French Queen Mother. Fearing the political influence of the populous Huguenots, Catherine persuaded her weak son, King Charles IX, to slay those who converged on the city to celebrate the royal wedding. Just days after the wedding, twenty-seven hundred Huguenots were slaughtered in the infamous St. Bartholomew Massacre. Pope Gregory XIII, jubilant at the carnage, prayed that this most Christian French king might purge his entire kingdom of the Huguenot plague.

Henry of Navarre saved his life by abjuring, although he returned to Protestantism just four years later in 1576. In 1589, after the assassination of King Henry III, Henry of Navarre was crowned King Henry IV—the first Protestant French king. With the crown on his head came a burden for his back—the Wars of Religion (1560–1598) between the Huguenots and Roman Catholics. Again displaying his talent for expedient action, he abjured and was thus able to restore peace once more. A Catholic again, he proclaimed the Edict of Nantes (in the castle of that western port city) in 1598—the first official recognition of religious toleration by a major European country. This legislation gave the Huguenots complete religious freedom in one hundred communities and the same civil rights as Roman Catholics.

The freedom did not last, however. After the 1610 assassination of King Henry IV, his widow became regent for their nine-year-old son, Louis XIII. The intelligent and energetic Cardinal Richelieu rose in power as the chief minister, ruling France from 1624 to 1642 in the interests of the minor king and his mother. To make royal power supreme, he reduced the independence of the feudal nobles and put down the rebellious Huguenots.

Persecution of the Huguenots accelerated in 1661 when the Sun King Louis XIV, sanctioned a series of proclamations reinterpreting the Edict of Nantes. A Catholic revival in France, plus the theory that the state would be more secure if all the king's subjects shared the same religion, led to heightened attempts to convert the Huguenots in 1678.

The Revocation of the Edict of Nantes, signed by the Sun King at Fontainebleau in 1685, triggered another wave of persecution. Two hundred thousand Huguenots emigrated over the next thirty years, draining France of its top artisans and merchants. They fled to England, Holland, Switzerland, Germany, America, and South Africa. Not until the Edict of Toleration two years before the 1789 French Revolution did Protestants receive their rights again.

The revocation stipulated that all Huguenot temples (churches) were to be destroyed immediately (around five hundred remained, and over three hundred had already been demolished). The stipulation was rigorously carried out. For example, the Charenton temple near Paris, designed by the architect Debrosses and serving a congregation of fourteen thousand, was levelled in five days. Unless they abjured, pastors had two weeks to leave the country or face hanging. Huguenot services were outlawed in any public place or private home. Huguenot children had to be baptized by Catholic priests and raised as Catholics or their parents were fined five hundred livres. Huguenots were strictly forbidden to leave the country—if they did, their property was confiscated. If caught fleeing the kingdom, women were sent to convents, for life, and men to the galleys, where they often died at the oarlock from overwork or disease.

The Roman Catholic clergy were so delighted with the legislation that choirs sang *Te Deum*s all across the country, processions were paraded from shrine to shrine, and Pope Innocent XI sent congratulations to King Louis XIV. In Paris, the king's portrait was painted, and a statue erected at the Hotel de Ville, the "bas-reliefs displaying a frightful bat, whose wings enveloped the books of Calvin."[3] Medals were struck to commemorate the extinction of Protestantism in France. In 1686, a clergyman wrote the following: "Great Louis, you have exterminated the heretics....The profane temples are destroyed, the pulpits of seduction are cast down, the prophets of falsehood are torn from their flocks. At the first blow dealt to it by Louis, heresy falls, disappears, [along with] its false gods, its bitterness, and its rage."[4]

One of the first sites of the Protestant movement was in Caen, where on June 25, 1685, the destruction of its temple by government decree began with the sound of trumpets, accompanied by shouts of the rabble of Caen. It didn't take them long to tear it down. Built in 1612, it was the only Protestant house of worship in France with a Roman Catholic-style belfry surmounted by a cross. Its large congregation had come from areas around the city; most of them were of a high social standing (ensuring that it was well subsidized).

Just three weeks before the destruction of Caen's temple, Louis

View of Caen, France, 1673. Tallest steeple is Saint Pierre with round chateau behind it.

Payzant's parents—Antoine Paisant and Suzanne Lecocq, both twen-ty-five—were married there. Antoine was a *drapier-chaussetier-mercier* (a merchant who sold fabric, hose, shoes, and supplies for tailors and dressmakers); his brothers were Caen merchants too.

One of Antoine's younger brothers, Jacques, had fled to England the year before, where he became a British citizen and a government translator. Because of his connections at Whitehall, Jacques (angli-cized to James) was able to use his influence to help Louis in the years to come.

The marriage contract of Louis' parents stated that from Suzanne's dowry of two hundred livres, sixty-six livres was for the wedding. As well as the cash dowry, her parents, (Pierre Lecocq and Anne Langlois), gave her a canopy bed with bed curtains of russet-coloured Caen serge (an expensive and highly esteemed fabric), bed linen, table linen, clothing (six shifts, a hoop, a black Camelot skirt), 40 pounds of pewter (probably plates), a table, cooking pots, a brass candlestick, and jewellery.[5] These details are a reminder of the wealth that many Huguenots were forced to leave behind upon fleeing France.

The Huguenots were subjected to another tactic by Louis XIV in his relentless persecution. In 1681, the Marquis de Louvois (1541–1691), the secretary of state for war and a harsh and violent man, told the district governor, or intendant, of Poitou that he was about to send troops into that province. "His Majesty," he wrote, "has heard with much joy of the great number of persons who continue to be converted in your department. He wishes you to persist in your endeavours, and desires that the greater number of horsemen and officers should be billeted upon the Protestants. If, according to a just distribution, ten would be quartered upon the members of the Reformed religion, you may order them to accommodate twenty."[6] This was the first use of the *dragonnades* (dragoons) in religious persecution—four years later, a truce freed up even more troops from active service.

Immediately after the 1685 revocation, the enforced billeting of dragoons in Protestant homes became more widespread. The ruthless soldiers made life miserable for the unwilling Huguenot hosts until they abjured—an effective method of forcible conversion. These troops were often recruited from the dregs of society: peasant boys, vagabonds, beggars, criminals, and sometimes German mercenaries. Governed by force and fear, and often with their pay in arrears, they looted and took what they wanted from the helpless Protestants.[7] The resulting mass conversions pleased the Crown and the pope.

In Caen, public authorities called together the leading Protestants in the town hall. The announcement on November 5, 1685, at 10:00 A.M. proclaimed that a royal regiment of sixteen hundred would soon arrive : the dreaded dragoons were on their way.[8]

Many Huguenots chose to flee the country rather than abjure. The French economy gradually declined due to wars, poor harvests, famines, and the exodus of Huguenots that had closed industries, depopulated villages, and left fields uncultivated. The famous Lyons silk industry was decimated. Of twelve thousand artisans, nine thousand fled to Switzerland and other countries. It took about a century for the French economy to be restored to its former prosperity.

Judith Mariengault, a young married woman, described her escape: "We quitted our home in the night, leaving the soldiers in their beds, and abandoning to them our home and all that it contained. Well knowing that we should be sought for in every direction, we remained ten days concealed in Dauphiny, at the house of a good woman, who had no thought of betraying us."[9] She and her family eventually reached America, via Germany, Holland, and London.

Jean Martheilhe, seventeen years old, was caught and imprisoned for attempting to reach Belgium. While awaiting his trial, five

Huguenot fugitives were brought in, captured by the dragoons. He recognized three gentlemen from his hometown, but not the other two, who, it turned out, were young women disguised as boys. They had attempted their winter escape through the Ardennes forest. They had travelled for about 30 leagues, or 120 kilometres, enduring cold, hunger and privations "with a firmness and constancy extraordinary for persons brought up in refinement, and who previous to this expedition would not have been able to walk a league."[10] The women were tried and sent to a Paris convent where they "wept out the rest of their lives and died."[11]

Jean, however, refusing to abjure, was condemned to the galleys. Marched in chains to Dunkirk with other prisoners, he endured twelve years of horrible hardships as a galley slave. Then, along with twenty-two others, all chained, he was marched through Paris and south to Marseilles to serve out the remainder of his sentence.[12]

Those Huguenots who chose to remain in France still found ways to practise their outlawed faith. The period between 1685 and 1789 was termed by the Huguenots the "Desert," referring to the trials of the Israelites in the Old Testament. Their Calvinist form of worship was severe and favoured the intellect rather than the emotions. Long sermons analyzed Christian doctrine. Appeals to the senses (colour, candles, and incense) were rigidly subdued. The minister wore a black gown instead of bright vestments, images of the Roman Catholic saints were destroyed, the sacraments were simplified, the service was conducted in French, and chanting replaced hymn singing.

Without temples, the Huguenots always met for services at night, and in secret locations—a wooded area, cave, rocky valley, or farm—anywhere that provided safe seclusion. They lit their way by oil lamps. The pastor carried a folding pulpit and his special tall hat (sometimes concealed by day under a milk churn). During the service,"men and women gathered in separate groups. Passages of scripture were read, psalms sung and a general confession was followed by a sermon. The service closed with a blessing and a collection for the poor. Elders were elected, psalters distributed and baptisms or marriages celebrated."[13]

At their services, Huguenots carried a *méreau*, a coin-like token shown to an elder to prove they were not Roman Catholic spies. Used for centuries, these tokens of pewter, lead, leather, wax, or glass were about thirty millimetres in diameter. One side often showed Christ as a shepherd standing in his flock blowing a horn and carrying a staff. On the obverse, a sun and six stars shone above an open Bible.[14]

Laws were passed that barred Huguenots from many middle-class

Rear of Saint-Pierre church by Odon River, ca. 1700s, Caen, France. Drawn by "Sam. Prout," engraved by "Jas. Carter."

Rear of Saint-Pierre church, Caen, France, 2001.

occupations: government administration, law, medicine, pharmacy, midwifery, bookselling, goldsmithing, and the selling of foodstuff.[15] It's no wonder so many Huguenots became successful merchants.

The Payzants, Antoine, Suzanne, and their son Louis, moved from the parish of Notre-Dame-de-Froiderue in 1720 and bought a house for three thousand livres in the St. Pierre parish. The house faced rue Saint-Pierre, and had a shop in front, kitchen behind, rooms above, and attic rooms above that. It backed onto a courtyard reached by a narrow passageway from the front street. On one side was rue des Goulets de St. Pierre, a street in the St. Pierre parish down which small rivulets flowed to the Odon River.

Louis' presumed birthdate of 1695 cannot be verified since the Protestant civil registers ended ten years earlier. Though Roman Catholic registers began in 1685 to list baptisms of Huguenots, identified as "born of the pretended marriage," the churches in Caen, along with the records, were destroyed in 1944. Duplicates at the Calvados Archives in Caen only start in 1737. Since Louis was of the age of majority (twenty-five, at least according to the laws in Paris[16]) in 1720 when he signed a document for the guild of *drapiers-chaussetiers*[17] he was probably born in 1695. He may have been living with his parents in 1723 when his father died at the age of sixty-three. At that time, his mother was described as a *marchande drapière-chaussetière*.

That same year, at twenty-eight, Louis married Anne-Marguerite Manson, twenty-five, who brought with her a substantial dowry of three thousand livres.

After the wedding, Louis' bride moved into the shop and house with him and his widowed mother. Perhaps all three worked in the business. Anne-Marguerite was a great help to her husband—a "Merchant of great property."[18] In 1724 a daughter, Suzanne, was born, then a son, possibly named Jacques.

The persecution touched the family personally—something that Louis had hoped would never happen. In 1734, when Suzanne was ten years old, several people abducted her and placed her in the Nouvelles Catholiques convent. Located about five blocks from Louis' home in Caen, the convent had been founded in 1658 by the bishop of Bayeux in order to create "New Catholics." Louis and Anne-Marguerite were devastated to lose their daughter in such a terrible way.

After the birth of another daughter, Anne, in 1737, Louis must have realized that his wife would not survive (possibly due to labour complications). Little Anne was sent away to a wet nurse and Louis hired someone to look after his ailing wife. Perhaps on the pretext of a business trip to London (then the most populous city in the world at 725,000)[19] in 1737 he spirited away his son Jacques, leaving him with his uncle Jacques (James). Since James was then seventy-two, Jacques may have been sent to live with one of his uncle's two married daughters. When James died in 1757 at the age of ninety-two, he left a small sum to "My Kinsman James Payzant" (i.e., young Jacques). The term "kinsman" often meant a nephew, in this case, a grandnephew.[20]

During this period in France, the middle-class bureaucrats, or intendants, were commissioned by King Louis XIV to govern the thirty-two districts into which France was divided for the administration of the will of the central government. Cities were divided into Roman Catholic parishes, each known by the name of the parish church. Intendants' duties were to ensure that the courts of justice were run according to the law, to raise money for the Crown, to maintain order and justice, and to promote prosperity for their district. By widening and paving roads, and lining country roads with trees, they also improved the system of roads. Sanitation was improved, and towns were embellished—some had lanterns hung at night on the streets.

Caen's intendant from 1727 to 1740 was Aubrey Félix, Marquis De Vastan. In a December 1731 report of his district's economy, he detailed aspects of the prominent fabric industry, describing various products, their composition, length, width, value, and the number of weavers and their earnings.[21] He was also in charge during the famines of 1737 and 1739. At a time when the price of bread was the determining factor in the French economy, some women, lucky enough to have bread for their tables, were murdered on the king's highway. The result: an uprising in Caen.[22]

De Vastan lived in the governor's residence on the grounds of the Caen château, mere blocks from where Louis Payzant lived and worked. Perhaps Louis sold him stockings or shoes, or fabric for his elegant suits. Anne-Marguerite died when daughter Anne was nine months old; she was buried in the ditch of the Caen château, "in the presence of Julien Paisant, *marchand-drapier-mercier* of the Froiderue parish"[23] (likely a Roman Catholic relative of Louis). Burials in Huguenot cemeteries were forbidden. By law, families had to declare the death to the civil and criminal authorities, but most did not (although Louis did). They buried loved ones in their gardens, in ditches around destroyed temples, or on the grounds of Huguenots with large properties.

This tragedy triggered the life-altering steps that Louis was to take. Four months after his wife's death, he wrote to the intendant, seeking the release of fourteen-year-old Suzanne from the convent. Dipping his quill in the ink pot, he wrote in a bold hand, forming the capital letters with flair:

> Your Grace, the Marquis De Vastan, Baron de vieux Pont,
> Counsellor to the King in his Councils, Master of Requests in his administration building, Intendant of Justice, Police and Finance in the generality of Caen.
>
> Louis Payzant, middle-class merchant of Saint Pierre of Caen, humbly beseeches,
>
> And relates to you that about four years ago, his daughter, being around ten years of age, was taken away by several people, and led to the Ladies of the new Converts. The supplicant suffered greatly since she would have been familiar with his business, [...and] last December 23, he suffered the loss of his Wife who was of great help to him, he is presently alone and has no one to assist him in his business, as well as comfort him in his sicknesses which occur very frequently, for which he will give medical proof if he was doubted. The supplicant was advised to offer you his request, if it is to your liking, Your Grace, to order that his daughter be returned to him, because she is also very sick, for her to be aware of what will be happening in the house. During her absence [from

the convent], she will fulfill her duty of Catholicity, and the above-mentioned Ladies of the prorogation will provide her with a director of conscience as they see fit, and will therefore give you Justice.

Presented in Caen this 20th March 1738

[signed formally] Paysant[24]

The intendant scribbled to the superior of the convent asking her advice. She replied:

Your Grace, since the daughter of Mr. Paysan has not yet done her first communion, and since we thought of having her do it by Easter, this will ease the leaving of the young girl, because of her good feelings, she seems to be very firm in the Catholic religion; she in fact requests of her father that, in the future, he should give her a Catholic servant.

Done in our community, this twenty-fifth March 1738

[signed] Sr. Soubretiere, Superior[25]

De Vastan requested that she have Louis write a submission at the convent. Louis' duress was evident in his cramped, yet clear, hand, as he wrote promises he did not believe in:

I submit myself to taking a servant in my home to be a help to my daughter, who is a Roman Catholic, approved by Mr. Vicaire, priest of St. Pierre of Caen, my parish, and this at the moment my daughter is brought back to me.

I promise to give her all the freedom to do her duties as a Roman Catholic, without any obstruction.

I agree that Mr. Vicaire, her priest, be her confessor and assist her into doing her first communion.

I promise that she will go twice a month to the Nouvelles Catholiques to hear the lectures of the two chaplain gentlemen.

I promise not to force her to see Protestants, and that she will not leave Caen without the authorization of his Grace the Intendant, in the faith of which I sign the present submission. Done in duplicate, this eighteenth April seventeen thirty-eight, in our community of the New Catholics.

[signed formally] Paysant[26]

After the superior of the convent witnessed and signed this submission, De Vastan added:

To the extent that the above-mentioned conditions are approved by Madam the Superior of the Nouvelles Catholiques, and to the extent that they are carried out, we consent that the daughter of

Louis Paysan be given back to her father.
Done in Caen, the 20th April 1738
[signed] De Vastan[27]

After one month's correspondence, Louis finally had his precious "Suzon" with him, albeit with strings attached. He was now a widower, with his son safely in London and his infant Anne still with a wet nurse. He probably had a relative keep Anne once she was weaned. Perhaps his seventy-eight-year-old mother still worked occasionally with him in the shop. It was at this time that he plotted his dangerous escape from France. He must have been an extremely devout Huguenot to leave behind the business he had inherited from his parents, when a simple abjuration would have allowed him to stay.

For the time being, he carried on his business as usual. On February 23, 1739, in the presence of a real estate lawyer, he signed a contract with his relative Marin Paisant, Sieur de la Motte, by which Marin would pay Louis an annual rent of sixteen livres for a property in the Caen royal fairgrounds.[28] By July 16, 1739, Louis had paid his servant Marie Lebailly sixty-two livres and a few sols.[29] Since the revocation of 1685 stipulated that Huguenots would be fined one thousand livres if they employed a Protestant servant, it's likely that she was Roman Catholic. Besides, the convent had ordered Louis to provide a Catholic servant for Suzanne the year before.

Reports of escapes from France show the Huguenots' determination to leave their homeland. Itineraries of escape routes were secretly distributed. One couple escaped to Holland disguised as orange sellers leading a donkey. Children were hidden in baskets slung across mules. Some fled on horseback at night and hid in the woods during the day. In their determination to flee, some women went to great lengths: cutting off their hair, darkening their faces, using ointments or juices to disfigure their skin, acting mentally deranged, or disguising themselves as servants pushing wheelbarrows through muddy roads.[30]

Passports were required to cross the heavily guarded borders, and recent Catholic converts were not allowed aboard ships or across borders without obtaining a special licence and posting bond for their return. Guards often recruited local peasants to be on the lookout for escapees, and troops were rewarded in proportion to their captives. Protestant masters of merchant ships from France, England, and Holland often hid escapees under bales of goods, heaps of coal or in empty casks until they left the harbour. All ports were well guarded. In one case, troops caught six children and sent them to the Caribbean as slaves.

To show that the troops meant business, captured adults were dragged along the town streets before being sent to the galleys or convents. By 1775, over three thousand men of all ages had been sent to the galleys.

A couple from Brittany attempted to escape separately—she made it to England, but he was arrested and imprisoned for attempting to leave the country as a *religionnaire fugitif* (fugitive for religious purposes). Refusing to abjure, he was tortured by being forced to stand on a heated iron floor that burned the flesh from his soles, rendering him a cripple. After years in prison, the grey-haired man managed to escape and made his way to London to search for his wife. Sent to a French immigrant's coffee house near Soho Square, he inquired about his wife, but with no luck. The grey-haired man didn't know it, but a travelling peddler seated in a corner overheard the description, and when he was next in Canterbury, inquired there. Fortunately the wife was found in that city working as a milliner. She presumed her husband had been sent to the galleys, or was long dead. She travelled to London where she found him hobbling on his crutches, and took him home to Canterbury.[31]

Another escape, according to a journal, had a happier ending. On October 5, 1685:

> I, David Garric, arrived at London, having come from Bourdeaux the 31st August, running away from the persecution of our Holy Religion. I passed through Saintonge, Poitou, and Brittany. I embarked at St. Malo for Guernsey, where I remained for the space of a month, leaving everything, even my wife and a little boy four months old, called Peter Garric, who was then out at nurse at the Bastide, near Bourdeaux.
>
> The 5th December, 1685…God gave me my wife at London. She embarked from Bourdeaux the 19th November, from whence she saved herself, and in a bark of 14 ton, being hid in a hole, and was a month upon sea with strong tempests, and at great peril of being lost and taken by our persecutors, who are very inveterate. Pray God convert them.
>
> The 22nd May, 1687—Little Peter arrived at London, by the grace of God, in the ship of John White, with a servant, Mary Mongorier, and I paid for their passage 22 guineas.[32]

False statements circulated in France claiming that ten thousand Huguenots who had escaped to England died of misery and that most of the survivors were pleading to return to France and abjure.[33]

Only about one-tenth of the Huguenots escaped France. Those who did left behind relatives, friends, and business associates. Contacts were maintained in many cases; for example, some emigrants became foreign representatives for French producers.

We know that Louis and his daughter Suzanne finally managed a successful escape from France, but there is no record of the route, the method, or the actual date, though it was probably between July 16 and September 19, 1739. They probably travelled overland from Caen southwest to the port at Granville, then by boat across to Jersey.

By September 19, 1739, they were safely in Jersey. That day Louis wrote four almost identical letters, three to colleagues in various towns in France, and one to a friend back in Caen. On December 14, all four letters were signed by auditors and again by Intendant De Vastan. The letters indicate that Louis had meticulously organized his affairs before his escape, and had considered the feelings of those he had left. To his colleagues he wrote:

Sir:

You will be surprised to learn that I left my hometown and my country to establish myself in foreign countries. I have not done this in order to harm anybody; I have left in funds, belongings and merchandise more than enough to pay off all my debts. You will find in the bottom of a cabinet, whose key is under the drawer in the same cabinet, on the side of the merchandise, a case with no lid, in which are the contracts that concern my business. You will find an account of what I owe and one of what is owed me. I only left on it the most important debts....

Please be so kind as to appoint as lawyers Mess. Aubert and des Bouillons, of Caen, for my business. I implore you Sir, to make as little expense as possible, as it would not be a credit. I do in all good conscience and with the most fairness possible. I have been scrupulous that I have left more than what I owed. Because, God help me if I had planned to harm someone, and reproach be brought upon me or my family. I was so far away from all of this that if I hadn't done what I did, I'd rather have sent packages from here, or pay interest until the payment is complete.

When you have settled the affairs, would you please send me a report, I keep a record of all the bills that concern me, due today. I beg you Sir, to render to us all justice, and to cause as little expense as possible, it is in your interest.

You will oblige the one who has the honour of being, with great esteem and consideration possible.

Your very humble and very obedient servant,
[signed] Louis Paysant[34]

Louis was now a religious fugitive who had escaped from France against the law. The inventory-taking of a fugitive's property was a vital part of the legal procedure. By October the authorities had placed seals on his shop and his home above it. (A seal was paper sealed with wax, placed over the doors to prevent anything from being disturbed or stolen.) The seals were broken in November for inventory, and for three days everything left by Louis was identified, listed, and evaluated, and his legal papers, including the request to De Vastan for Suzanne's release, seized. Everything inventoried was left in the care of Louis' mother.

Every one of the 360 bolts of fabric left in his shop was measured, described, and evaluated. (Louis' merchandise and furniture totalled 2,500 livres). Measurement was by the *aune* (slightly longer than a metre), a standard that was dropped when the metric system was adopted after the French Revolution. *Camelot, dauphine, droguet, grenade, noisette,* and *pinchina* (to name a few of the fabrics) were made from wool, linen, and cotton in various colours and textures. Although they were mostly intended for clothing, these fabrics were also used for bedding, table linens, and curtains for beds and windows. Many of the bolts were identified by the name of the merchants who were to reclaim them.

Items of clothing from Louis' merchandise included four pairs of hose wrapped in black buckram (a lining used to stiffen clothes); twenty-two pairs of breeches ranging in size from large to small, all wrapped in grey buckram; and eight pairs of buttoned gaiters wrapped in black buckram. There were no shoes listed, perhaps because he had sold them all and did not re-order any because he knew he was leaving. Tailoring and dressmaking supplies included various lengths, widths, and colours of ribbon; four sheepskins for lining breeches; cotton thread; tape; buckram; and 96 dozen buttons.

Some items from the shop were a counter with two drawers containing scissors, keys, and a wicker basket of coins (69 livres, 5 sols, and 1 liard); a bench; four caned chairs; two stools; a writing chest; and a leather pouch containing sixteen small pieces of fabric in different colours (possibly fabric samples), and a tailoring, or dressmaking, mannequin.

Household items included table linen; two folding tables; a candlestick; six caned chairs; a woven rug; oil cruet; salad bowl, plates, and a mustard pot, all faience (Norman earthenware decorated with opaque-coloured glazes); a metal box containing tea; a sugar grater; pewter salt-cellar; six glasses; teacups and saucers; seven earthenware pots; forty-two fine pewter plates (likely from his mother's dowry), and twenty-two earthenware plates on a wooden dresser; andirons, fire tongs, and bellows; kitchen utensils in brass, iron, and bronze; tin lanterns; armoires; white linen window curtains; child's wicker cradle; eighty books; and two small birdcages. The bed frame had wood-turned posts, four bed curtains at the head, a valence covered with blue linen and trimmed with yellow chenille and ribbon. On the bed were three mattresses (of straw, feathers, and probably wool), a woolen blanket, quilt, two pillows and their cases, and a bolster. Louis had a duchess bed, which he may have inherited from his parents.

Since book-collecting was a popular hobby in eighteenth-century France,[35] Louis may have inherited some of his library from his father, who had lived on Notre-Dame-de-Froiderue, formerly a street of printers. The ordinary classes had few books, though clerics and members of the leisure class owned more. A noble might have thirty books; in 1760 Governor General Vaudreuil of New France had only fifteen. Poor Louis had had to leave behind a considerable collection.

Personal items in the inventory included a pair of beaver shoes with gold ribbon (Anne-Marguerite's, most likely); a muff with its belt and buckle in a cardboard box; two empty square scent bottles; eleven women's shifts; a mirror; walking cane; man's night shift; six neck bands and eight cravats; two pairs of cotton stockings in a wicker basket; velvet vest and breeches; flannel dressing gown; a blue fabric garment bag with white silk braid; handkerchiefs; two hats, a wig and wool hat in a chest; two small white camisoles; a child's worn shift; and a small woolen vest.[36]

Twenty-eight serviettes and twenty-five hand towels were in such a bad state that they were all sent out to be laundered during the taking of the inventory.

The legal process against Louis gathered momentum. By December 5, 1739, the king's attorney had drawn up his prosecution address and decided to conduct an investigation. The address read:

> The King's Attorney who has been informed that against and to the prejudice of the Edicts and Declarations of the King issued in August 1669, May 18 and July 14, 1682, October 1685, May 7, 1686, February 11 and September 13, 1699, Louis Paisant *chaussetier drapier* of this town left the kingdom three months ago, without authorization, because of religion and that he even abducted his children to pass through to foreign lands with the goal of settling there. As this departure and abduction fall precisely within the King's above-mentioned Edicts and Declarations which rule that a trial be carried out and perfect to those who act in such a way that

they must be punished according to the rigor of the Laws; which allows him [the attorney] to request that he be allowed to lead an extraordinary investigation against the above-mentioned Louis Paysant by way of letters and witness accounts as well as by the censure of the Church to prove that the above-mentioned Louis Paisant withdrew without permission from this kingdom to settle in foreign countries and to have withdrawn his daughter using false promises from the *Nouvelles Catholiques* of this town in view of taking her to foreign countries, and that a few years ago he even took his son then very young, to settle in the above-mentioned foreign countries, all of that without authorization and because of a religious issue.

Deliberated this [blank] December 1739,
[signed] Le Courtois.[37]

The evidence cited as "letters" no doubt referred to the four sent from Jersey, and the "censure of the Church" meant Louis' request to De Vastan for Suzanne's release.

Days later, six people were summoned to appear in court as witnesses, including several merchants (though no relatives), a lawyer, and Louis' servant, Marie Lebailly.[38] As for Louis' vacant shop and home, on Christmas Day in 1739, a merchant, Perrotte, was allowed to rent the premises at an annual rate of 120 livres for a minimum of six years.

By January, an agent acting on behalf of Louis' creditors began the process of listing and selling the furniture, personal effects, and merchandise. A year and a half later, the agent requested and received legal permission to sell Louis' three properties to pay outstanding debts.

In September 1741, for three consecutive weeks, the agent and his associates spoke after mass in three different parish churches (those that included Louis' properties). They read a proclamation identifying the properties to be auctioned off, as well as the location and date of the sale. Then they posted placards on the main doors of those churches and also at the market, main crossroads, and other public locations to ensure that the townspeople were made aware of the sale.

At the auction, the opening bid for Louis' shop and home was twelve hundred livres. Of the five bidders, two were relatives: Louis' uncle, Jean Paisant, and Marin Paisant (bidding may have been restricted to Roman Catholics). The final bid, 2,050 livres, was from Pierre-François Lieux, sieur des Jardins, the father of Louis' friend and neighbour, Pierre Lieux.

A property on rue Vaugueux that Louis had leased seventeen years earlier sold for 750 livres. Louis had leased it for for forty livres annually to a chef at the tavern Soleil. There was no contest for the Caen fairgrounds property that Louis had leased to Marin Paisant two years earlier. It sold for four hundred livres.[39]

The government took over two years to settle Louis' estate. All the legal costs—the placing of the seals, inventory-taking, the trial, investigation, and auction—were no doubt deducted from the final property sales.

As for his family, little Anne was probably raised by relatives in Caen, as she would have been too young to risk escape. Louis' son, Jacques, lived in England and his daughter, Suzanne, was with him in Jersey. Suzanne Payzant , Louis' mother, died at the age of ninety in 1750. (After Jean-Samuel Paisant, *marchand mercier* of the Froiderue parish, obtained authorization, she was buried in the garden of Bacon, sieur de Précourt, in the St. Saveur parish.)[40] It is not known whether she ever abjured, or was as strong an adherent to the Reformed faith as her son.

CHAPTER TWO

Jersey, Island of Refuge
(1739–1753)

Louis and fifteen-year-old Suzanne may have travelled in disguise from Caen overland to Granville on Normandy's west coast. From there, they would have taken a small boat fifteen kilometres to one of the Huguenan Islands, and then transferred to a more seaworthy boat to complete the trip to their safe haven—the island of Jersey. (Part of the French-owned Chausey Islands, the three small, windswept, and deserted Huguenan Islands—two disappear at high tide—were named for the Huguenots who changed boats there.)

"I happily arrived with Suzon, my dear daughter," Louis wrote, "after having gone through a rough storm and having seen the sea over the sides of our boat, but thanks to the Good God it was a good and big well-built boat, because if it hadn't been, we would all have perished. We were nine passengers. I was the only one who wasn't seasick, which gave me some grief since I had to work at maneuvering like the sailors."[1] He was likely exhausted by the perilous voyage and the months of secret preparations beforehand, and relieved to have landed safely.

For Louis, the total freedom to practise his own religion, assume civil rights, and practise a profession must have been worth the pain of leaving his family, possessions, business, and familiar surroundings. But it was more than that. "The reason for my departure," he wrote a colleague, "was my daughter who I took with me, she being four years in a convent. She was returned to me after the death of my dear wife under such difficult and terrible circumstances that they still make me tremble. You will see in the statement that I left with my other papers that I do not lie to you. I would sometimes hear very softly that if the smallest thing was discovered, they would take my daughter back, and let me rot in prison."[2]

Jersey was a popular place of Huguenot refuge, as Calvinism had been practised there from its inception two centuries earlier. Being a small island, it was a vast change for Louis from the gentle rolling hills of Lower Normandy. Jersey, the largest of the Channel Islands, is 117 square kilometres, only 24 kilometres from France, and 161 kilometres from mainland England. Louis would have appreciated the mild winters and long summers due to Jersey's Gulf Stream location. Canted towards the south, the island slopes gently from the north coast, which is edged by steep pink granite cliffs. The south coast is bordered by flat sandy beaches interspersed with rocky outcrops. Strong tides, treacherous currents, and fog make sea travel hazardous around Jersey. Tidal currents there are among the strongest in the world, and huge areas of offshore reefs and rocky islets are exposed at low tide.

When Louis arrived, Jersey's connection with England already spanned half a millennium. It dated from one of the most pivotal points in English history—the Norman Invasion. When the French Duke of Normandy conquered England in 1066, he already owned the Channel Islands, which included Jersey. In the thirteenth century, France regained Normandy, but failed to get the Channel Islands. The islanders were allowed to retain their French language and customs, but owed allegiance to the British crown (though not to the British parliament).

In 1739, Jersey's capital of St. Helier had about two thousand inhabitants living in four hundred houses, a much smaller population than in Caen. St. Helier (named after the sixth-century hermit who brought Christianity to the island), is on the south coast, on the east side of St. Aubin's Bay.

Louis likely felt optimistic about his prospects because the town was well-established and prosperous, as indicated in a 1734 description:

> All round on the North quarters it is fenced against cold blasts by hills rising up gradually into the Island. From the bottom of those hills to the Town lies a flat of meadows, watered by a clear stream, which, after it has enriched them, enters the Town, runs along some of the streets, under some of the houses, so that by a bucket let down through a trap-door the water is brought up with the greatest ease....
>
> The Town is inhabited chiefly by merchants, shop-keepers, artificers, and retailers of liquors; the landed gentlemen generally

living upon their estates in the country. In short, here is scarce anything wanting for necessity or convenience.[3]

A busy port in 1731, St. Helier had seventeen boats specializing in the Newfoundland-Jersey cod fishery alone. That trade had only begun to prosper a year earlier (after a century of fluctuations) and continued until the French Revolution in 1789.

The Channel Islanders "had connections with Newfoundland from a very early date. An old tradition maintains that Jerseymen, while on their way to Iceland to engage in the fishery, were overtaken by a strong wind which drove them southwest until they reached a land, the waters around which were filled with fish. This land was believed to be Newfoundland. Cabot made his voyage shortly after,"[4] in 1497.

A century later Jerseymen joined a larger group of fishing vessels from the west coast of England to fish the cod-rich waters off Newfoundland, from March to September each year. William Pitt the Elder (1708-1778) claimed that the "Grand Cod Fishery of the Universe [was] a more inexhaustible and infinitely more valuable source of Wealth than all the mines in the World."[5] Split, salted and dried in the sun, cod was a relatively light-weight, protein-rich and well-preserved foodstuff ready for shipping to European ports. During the fishing season, cod was sold or traded to masters of visiting ships for staples such as sugar, molasses, rum, flour, tea, livestock, tobacco, woollen cloth, boots, shoes, and fishing equipment and supplies.

The Newfoundland fishery became dependent on the English and Jersey shipping industries. Vessels had to be outfitted, and food, clothing, and fishing equipment assembled. Ships often had room for paying passengers (usually fishermen) at £3 per passenger (one way), and 20 shillings per ton for supplies and provisions. Great fortunes were made in the port cities of the west country of England, in Jersey, and the emerging Newfoundland settlements.

In the St. Helier harbour, ships imported wine, brandy, and fruit from France, Spain, Portugal, and Italy, and exported them to America, Brazil, and the West Indies. Tobacco was imported from Virginia. (Sir Walter Raleigh, governor of Jersey from 1600 to 1603, may have introduced the custom of smoking to Jersey).

One of the first items on Louis' agenda was to write home. He addressed one of the letters to "Monsieur Pierre Lieux Marchand Sur Les goullets St. Pierre a Caen." Pierre Lieux, sieur des Jardins, was a friend, merchant, and former neighbour.

I am honoured to write to you from Jersey. If I did not say good-bye, my very dear friend, it is that I had reasons. Forgive me if I left in the manner that I did, I did not intend to cause anyone harm....Suzon sends her love to Marotte from her heart and myself likewise....There is in my cabinet 62 livres and a few sols in a bag, with a bill stating that it belongs to my servant, that I left an account for her....Please be assured of my very humble respects, Mr. and Mrs. Des Jardins, as well as Mr. and Mrs. Ruel, that I will have the honour of writing them, when my affairs afford me more time.

Your very humble and very obedient servant,
[signed] Louis Paysant[6]

As a fugitive, Louis could never return to Caen to see his widowed seventy-nine-year-old mother or his two-year old daughter, Anne. Before he fled, Louis had provided for his mother financially and no doubt had relatives take care of her, as he had done for his daughter. Still, it couldn't have been easy for him to know he could never see them again.

At the age of forty-four, Louis had decisions to make, and he may have had relatives on the island to help him. There is a record of a Susanne Paisant, wife of Caen merchant Robert Badentrop, who abjured in 1690 in the parish of Trinity, Jersey—in other words, she reverted back to Protestantism after abjuring to the Catholic Church in Caen.[7] She could have been Louis' aunt, his father's sister.

Louis would have to restart a business, and plan for Suzanne's future. He would also need a wife and helpmate. Since he married four months after moving to Jersey, perhaps he already had someone in mind before he left Caen—someone he was in love with, or who shared a business background. She would be a woman who could give him another family.

His wife-to-be, Marie Anne Noget, was a fellow Huguenot, also from Normandy. Born in 1711, she was a native of the town of Condé in Lower Normandy,[8] and fled to the Island of Jersey "as a young woman."[9] She may have escaped the Huguenot persecution hidden in a cart west-bound for Granville, or perhaps she walked the distance dressed as a peasant, with family or friends. She would have joined other Huguenots for the sea journey to Jersey.

Whether Louis met her first in Normandy or Jersey, their connection might have come from the fabric trade, since Condé sur-Noireau was known for its textile industry. They may also have had family or Huguenot connections. Perhaps Marie Anne's father had been in the weaving business in Condé-sur-Noireau. She may have accompanied him north to Caen, selling to merchants, Louis being among them. Louis would have been a major customer, because in 1739 he had hundreds of bolts of fabric in his shop (some known to be from Condé). Or perhaps Louis travelled to various cities and towns purchasing fabric and met her in Condé.

Marie Anne's hometown was centuries old when she was born. Early Romans named it from the Latin verb *condere*, meaning "to build" or "to found."[10] There, the Druance River merges with the Noireau (blackwater), the river that eventually joins the Odon and flows northward through Caen to the English Channel. Condé had been an industrial centre for centuries, including cutlery manufacturing, and leather tanning from sheep and cow hides.[11] The largest industry by far was textiles: by 1731, it supported two-thirds of Condé's three thousand residents.[12] There were 250 busy looms, most in private homes in the countryside and some in town factories, with overseers from Caen. Spinners (usually women and children who drew out and twisted fibres from sheep fleece, or cotton, linen, or hemp) earned three to four sols daily, while weavers (usually men) earned twice as much.[13]

Droguet Condé cinq lames,[14] a wool drugget woven in Condé, with five gold or silver metallic threads woven through it, was listed among Louis Payzant's stock in 1739. This fabric was often used for men's waistcoats, which, at that time, ended just above the knee.

Like her future bridegroom, Marie Anne's surname indicates that she was a member of the bourgeoisie. (A list of the bourgeoisie in seventeenth-century Condé includes the names Lecocq and Langlois—the surnames of Louis Payzant's maternal grandparents.)[15] This middle class, between the lords and the vassals, enjoyed special rights and privileges in Condé society. They had the right to pass freely on several town bridges without having to pay a toll to the seigneur for maintenance and repair. On Mondays and Thursdays, they could display their merchandise at the market under covered stalls and pay a reduced fee. They also had the privilege of fishing in the Noireau and Druance rivers using a fishing line or a mesh net with holes at least as big as a man's thumb. And they could hunt with a stick and hunting dogs (though still without a gun) on all the land surrounding Condé.

As with Louis in Caen, Marie Anne grew up in an environment plagued by the Huguenot-Catholic conflict. The Protestant movement reached Condé-sur-Noireau in the 1570s. Services held within the walls of the château[16] and presided over by the minister, Mr. Berthelot, attracted people from surrounding villages. Twenty years later the

Ancient Condé house, Grande-Rue, Condé-sur-Noireau, France, ca. sixteenth century.

seigneur of the château forbade the congregation to meet there because he didn't want meetings on his wife's property. The congregation then assembled north of Condé in a marshy, barren field. In 1603, they built straw huts for protection from the winter cold. A proper temple wasn't built until 1629.[17]

The only remaining record of the temple's activities is from 1678. That year Samuel de Brais conducted twenty-five baptisms, four marriages, and eight burials for his flock of one thousand. Baptisms listed the parents' names, with the mother's in her maiden name according to the custom. Most parishioners were bourgeois and included writers, merchants, apothecaries, and a physician. Burials took place in the cemetery next to their temple, or in a Huguenot cemetery in the St. Martin parish of the southern part of Condé.

In 1680 the temple was destroyed by government decree, forcing the adherents to meet in private homes. Five years later, after the revocation, one hundred Protestants in Condé abjured in merely three weeks of occupation by the dragoons.[18]

There are records of several members of the passionately Protestant Manson family in Condé-sur-Noireau. (Louis Payzant's first wife was a Manson.) Nicholas Manson refused to convert in 1685. In the early 1700s, brothers Pierre and Jacob Manson, were linen manufacturers and bourgeois merchants in Condé. Mathieu Manson allowed secret burials in his vineyard on rue du Vieux-Château in Condé.[19] In 1731 Sieur Binard wanted to lock his wife and his sister-in-law in a convent because they were taking religious instruction from the same Mathieu Manson.[20]

A municipal department in Condé was specifically concerned with the collection of goods left behind by the religious fugitives. Around the time of Marie Anne's flight, there were still five hundred Huguenots in Condé.

Although we don't know exactly how Louis and Marie Anne met, we do know they were married. The wedding of Louis Payzant, forty-five, and Marie Anne Noget, twenty-nine, took place at the St. Helier Parish Church, Jersey, on January 20, 1740, four months after Louis arrived (and two years after Anne-Marguerite had died).

"Mr. Louis Paisant and Miss Anne Noget," reads the original marriage entry in French, "both from the Province of Normandy were married together [this] twentieth day of January 1738, by Monsieur Rodolphe Hue, Officiating Minister, and by the courtesy of the Venerable François Payn, Dean of the Island of Jersey."[21] However, a clerical error, the fact that different calendars were used in Jersey and France, and the fact that Louis was still in France in February 1739, indicate that 1738 is incorrect. It was more likely 1740 when they were married.

They were married not by the resident minister of that church, Pierre Daniel Tapin, but by Rodolphe Hue, rector of St. Brelade Parish (west of St. Helier), requiring them to seek permission from François

Inside the Parish Church of St. Helier, Jersey, Channel Islands, 2001.

Payn, dean of Jersey, who supervised the twelve Church of England parishes on the island.

I believe the clerk who wrote the marriage entry made an error and should have written "1739," because there are nine other entries all dated 1739 on the page headed "Anno 1739."

Also, at that time Britain and France used different calendars. The Julian calendar used by Britain did not accurately reflect the solar year, and by the eighteenth century that calendar had fallen eleven days behind real astronomical time. Another component of the Julian calendar was that the New Year began on March 25. Britain (including Jersey) didn't switch to the Gregorian calendar used by European countries until 1752. Assuming the clerical error, Louis and Marie Anne's wedding date was January 20, 1739. Since that date falls between January 1 and March 24 on the Julian calendar, today it would be transcribed as "1739/40" (known to genealogists as "double-dating") and interpreted as "1740" in our modern Gregorian calendar. (France had been using the Gregorian calendar since 1564, so Louis and Marie Anne must have thought this difference of three months was a step backward.)

The overwhelming evidence for the date error is that Louis signed a legal document in Caen in February 1739, making it impossible for him to have been in Jersey the previous month. He would only have made his perilous escape once, and that was in September 1739.

With his knowledge of the latest styles in fabrics and shoes, and the quality of the local tailors' designs, Louis probably had an appropriate wedding gown made for his bride, though not in white (a nineteenth-century custom). He would have selected a fine pair of shoes for her from his stock (assuming he was in business by then), most likely imported from England. They would have had a thick curved heel—shaped high heels were worn only by upper-class men and women—covered with fabric, and a slightly pointed, upturned toe. Unlike today, eighteenth-century shoes were identical for both the left and right foot. These formal shoes were likely made of damask, a firm lustrous fabric, with two wide straps over the instep, which threaded through a large silver buckle. Since tradition states that the shoes were silver,[22] they would have been made of a silver fabric, or a coloured fabric with shiny silver threads throughout, or covered with silver ornaments.

They were married in a church built in the eleventh century. At one time its cemetery walls were so close to the sea shore that waves washed against them at high tide in spring. By the 1700s the water had receded, leaving the church near the heart of town. Parts of the building were constructed in different periods out of various materials such

The parish church of St. Helier, Jersey, Channel Islands, ca. 1993.

as rough beach boulders, grey granite quarried from the nearby Chausey Islands and, predominantly, local pink granite.

The church was much more than just a centre of worship. Its square tower, built circa 1450, served as a beacon to mariners. The tower's bell was the town's key piece of communications technology. It announced the opening of the Saturday market in the nearby square, summoned the people to the defense of their homes against enemy or pirate attacks, reported fire alarms, and announced the meeting of the parish assembly. The stocks at the churchyard gate were used to punish those who spoke disrespectfully of officials, were found drunk, or disobeyed even minor municipal ordinances. The church stored the militia's arms and cannon, the municipal treasures, and a cache of grain to ensure against starvation.

The Jersey church was originally Roman Catholic, with authority from Coutances, Normandy, then from Salisbury, England. During the sixteenth-century Reformation, authority switched to the Diocese of Winchester in England. When the British Crown decreed that all objects of Roman Catholic superstition were to be eliminated,

Jerseymen obeyed, smashing stained glass windows, statuary and fonts, and whitewashing the walls and ceilings.[23]

French Huguenot ministers began preaching in Jersey in 1562, when John Calvin appointed one of his pupils from Geneva as rector of the St. Helier church. As a Huguenot temple, it featured a three-decker pulpit surrounded by a haphazard collection of family pews and seven galleries, including one for smokers. The minister and elders, somberly clothed in black, celebrated Holy Communion once every quarter. When it was needed, a silver dish used as a baptismal bowl was set on the communion table in front of the pulpit.

Baptismal records of the St. Helier Parish Church reveal that the godparents of Marie Anne and Louis' children were all of high social standing, likely an indication of Louis' success as a merchant in his new community. The Payzants followed the custom of naming each child after its godparent of the same sex. All but one were so named.

Marie Anne and Louis had seven children baptized at the church from November 1740 to July 1751. Unfortunately, by 1746 their first three had been buried in the parish cemetery. Jean Louis died in 1744 at age three. Marie and Anne were buried on the same day, April 10, 1746, at age five and three. Their deaths might have been from smallpox or some other epidemic, or perhaps they were killed at the same time in an accident.

The honour of being godparents to Marie Anne and Louis' firstborn, Marie (1740–1746), went to Louis' seventy-five-year-old uncle, Jacques (James) Payzant, and his wife, Marie le Vasson, who lived in London and were guardians of Louis' son Jacques. Unable to be at the baptism, they were represented by local friends.

Jean and Anne Vivien, friends from Caen, were godparents to the first son, Jean Louis (1741–1744), and they too were represented by locals: a "gentleman and officer of the garrison" and his daughter. Other godfathers included a parish constable (one of twelve in the States Assembly, the island's legislative body), a court writer (or municipal clerk), and other "gentlemen."

Louis' son Jacques spent some time in Jersey, but returned to London to live with his father's uncle. Suzanne didn't stay long in Jersey either—by the time she was eighteen, she too was in London. In a letter dated October 1742 to his uncle in London, Louis expressed displeasure with the behaviour of his son (then possibly aged ten):

> It has been ten days since I wrote to my son where I tell him that you are unhappy with him, that he is disrespectful to his master and mistress and that you wrote to me about it. I exhort him to

become more submissive and to better fulfill his duty, and that he follow your advice, as well as that of Madame your wife. I beg you, Sir, to please continue with him.

I requested Monsieur Hue, minister, who was his teacher here, to see him and show him that he will draw the hatred of people who take an interest in him, and that I am not happy with him. Monsieur Hue promised to tell him when he is in London.[24]

Louis sent his uncle £21, 11 shillings and 7 sols, to pay "what is due for my son's illness." He also asked his uncle to advise him what he owed for his son's allowance. He apologized: "Forgive me, Sir, for all the sorrows and annoyances that I cause you."

Expressing delight in his two-year old daughter (Marie), Louis penned: "Our little Malet has the honour to present you and Madame your wife, as well as your dear family, her very humble respects." Louis sent two aprons to London (via a Madame Guillet) for Suzanne and two handkerchiefs for Jacques: "I ask you, Sir, to have the goodness to have him use them." Departing from domestic matters, Louis noted: "We have received here some news that the Spanish sank a brigantine from New England which left from here about three months ago."

Louis possibly resumed running a retail operation as he had in France, or he may have become involved in shipping as a commission agent, perhaps in the lucrative Newfoundland trade. Since privateering was practically a business at that time (even local Jerseymen were privateers), St. Helier merchants were no doubt relieved when their ships returned from English ports with cargoes intact. The English Channel "swarmed with pirates of all nationalities and the doughty little Jersey vessels had often all their work cut out to evade falling into their hands."[25]

Louis probably rented a house in St. Helier (there are no records of his purchasing or selling property) and carried out his business from a store front on the ground floor, with living quarters upstairs. As the town was quite small, the French Huguenot community was close-knit, probably living around the Royal Square at the centre of town, and on nearby streets.

In his shop, Louis sold a popular type of warm stockings that were made from the spun wool of Jersey sheep and knitted by the locals. (He may have exported them too.) The secret of these comfortable stockings was the knit, which allowed them to stretch and return to their original shape—the basic stitch known today as the "jersey" stitch. Due to high demand throughout Europe, the manufacture of stockings was the principal industry in Jersey during the sixteenth and seventeenth centuries.

The upper class favoured silk stockings, but occasionally they wore woolen ones. In fact, in 1586 Mary, Queen of Scots, sentenced to death for treason by her half-sister Queen Elizabeth I, wore a pair of white Jersey hose to her execution, covered by a second pair in sea-blue with a silver design. At least her legs were warm.

Men, women, and children of all classes in Jersey took up the popular occupation of knitting, but by law had to stop during harvest and "vraicing" (pronounced "wracking")—the gathering of seaweed for manure—or face imprisonment in the castle on a diet of bread and water.

Women knitted while riding to market, fishermen knitted stockings or waistcoats while the fish were biting, and people even took their knitting to church, where the clicking of the needles was said to drown the preacher's voice. During long winter evenings, neighbours would gather in each other's homes for knitting parties known as *veilles* (staying up at night), during which they "sang songs and told stories of olden time, of ghosts and of witches, thus beguiling the irksomeness of their task."[26] At one time six thousand pairs of stockings were knitted per week, then sold at the market to delighted merchants who scrambled to export them to various European ports. Louis personally exported eighty dozen pairs to Nova Scotia in 1753.

A contemporary description of Jersey's market states that it was held "every Saturday...in the Towne of St. Helery...all the year long [with] all commodities in the manner of a Faire."[27] The weekly event drew a flood of people from all parts of the island to conduct business and trade gossip in this country-fair atmosphere. At the market cross, officials read all public proclamations, and from the cross the distances to all the milestones on the island were measured. On the south side of the square was the granite Royal Court House, built in 1648. Around the corner to the east, the Jersey parliament sat in session at the States Chambers, and to the west could be found St. Helier Parish Church.

A public library opened in 1743 not far from the market square, thanks to an endowment from the native historian Reverend Philippe Falle. Louis, having left eighty books behind in Caen, was no doubt pleased to have something to read again.

A great ceremony took place in St. Helier that Louis and Marie Anne wouldn't have missed. In the summer of 1751, a gilded lead statue of King George II was dedicated in the centre of the marketplace, probably on the spot of the old market cross. The statue had been erected in gratitude for the king's contribution of £300 towards the completion of a much needed harbour.

To mark the unveiling of the statue, a parade of almost 250 soldiers and 30 mounted troops entered the market square with swords drawn, trumpets blaring, and drums setting the march time. Government officials, military officers, and the clergy followed. After a drum roll, the wooden case was removed to reveal the golden statue of the sixty-eight-year-old king dressed as a Roman emperor. The unveiling ceremony took place on July 9, 1751, and "was an occasion of great military and civic splendour culminating in the proclamation by the Deputy-Viscount 'that this statue is erected in honour of His Sacred Majesty King George the Second whom God long preserve to reign over us,' followed by a signal from the top of the church to the castle, where a suitable salute was fired. The Market Place was renamed [Royal Square] in honour of the King, but for many years was referred to as *le marchi* [the market] or *le vier march* [the old market]."[28]

After the proclamation, the crowd gave three cheers, the militia responded to the Royal Salute from Elizabeth Castle and everyone toasted the king's health. In the evening, a great bonfire on the hill, the Mont de la Ville, illuminated the whole town.

The lavish festivities celebrating the king's gift and its potential economic impact on Jersey must have greatly pleased Louis, who as a merchant and perhaps a ship owner would have recognized the need for an improved harbour. He and Marie Anne likely drank to the king's health with great appreciation for their blessings. Louis certainly had plenty to be happy about—he had tasted freedom of conscience, excelled in renewing his business, and was pleased with his new young family (Phillip, four; Mary, three; John, one; and newborn Lewis).

Every successful entrepreneur is always on the lookout for new opportunities, so Louis would have been quick to pick up the stories circulating at the time about new prospects in the British colony of Nova Scotia. Halifax had been established in Nova Scotia in 1749, but Nova Scotia's Governor Cornwallis, dissatisfied with the British immigrants who had settled there, wrote to London requesting more immigrants, especially Protestants from the German states and Switzerland. The British government was reluctant to send more settlers from England, as it was not overpopulated, and besides, there were many other available Protestants unhappy with their situation in Europe.

In December 1749, an advertisement circulated in London (and probably Jersey) describing Nova Scotia in glowing details: "the Climate is as healthy, and the Soil as Rich and fertile as any other of the British colonies…the Seacoast abounds with Fish in greater plenty and variety than any other part of America and is peculiarly adapted to Commerce and Navigation...The Inland parts are very proper for the cultivation and Produce of Grain, Hemp, Flax."[29]

People like Louis learned of Britain's desire to send several hundred French Huguenots from Jersey to settle in Nova Scotia. There were some restrictions, though. Prospective settlers had to have a useful trade and employment, be able to provide a recommendation by one or more persons of credit or reputation, and not be manufacturers. The latter were discouraged because Britain desired a colony that would supply raw materials and provide a market for manufacturers. Not many Huguenots applied, however, and several of those who did were reputed to be manufacturers. But Louis' business fit Britain's desired model exactly, as he likely planned to buy English goods for resale to settlers in Nova Scotia or Newfoundland.

Louis recognized a significant opportunity for his business, and potential for his four children in a new land. But he must also have had a sense of adventure to give up his very comfortable and well-established life in St. Helier for the unknown in new territory.

In April 1753, Louis acquired a formal letter of recommendation, a first-class entrée into the new world, from John Pownall in London, secretary to the Lords of Trade and Plantations. This government organization of gentlemen in Whitehall, commissioned in November 1748, had a lengthy title: "Commissioners for promoting the Trade of this Kingdom and for inspecting and improving his Majesty's plantations in America and elsewhere."[30] Generally known as the "Board of Trade," its purpose was primarily to investigate and advise. No doubt Louis was able to obtain the letter through his uncle, Jacques (James), who was a translator in the office of the Secretary of State, the body to which the Board of Trade reported.

Not having to plan a covert departure this time, Louis had sufficient time to organize his leave. In 1753 he, with his family and effects, sailed out of St. Helier, leaving the island of Jersey behind forever and looking forward eagerly to great success in the new world. "[He] moved over to Nova Scotia with a great property, in order to Make a fortune for himself and his children."[31]

According to "A List of Ships and Vessels which have entered Inwards in the Port of Halifax in the Province of Nova Scotia between Lady Day [March 25] and Michaelmas [Sept. 29] 1753,"[32] only one ship arrived from Jersey that summer: the thirty-ton brigantine *Mary*, which docked on July 20, 1753. Historian Mather Byles DesBrisay wrote in 1870 that Louis "owned three vessels in Jersey, where he sold two, and...he came in the third with his family to Halifax."[33] However,

Dedicated to my mother
Mary Marie Louise Nazette Layton (née Payzant),
the first Mary Payzant I knew

Acknowledgements

I couldn't have written this book without the love, support, encouragement, guidance, and assistance of so many.

Thanks to Aunt Gussie (Augusta West, née Harlow) of Toronto for giving me an 1884 tintype, a year before she died at ninety-two in 1962.

My mother and father, Mary and Bob Layton of St. Catharines, Ontario, have been constantly enthusiastic and supportive.

Barry Botsford of Vancouver sent me the magazine article in 1985 that first inspired me to write about Marie Anne and Louis. Joyce Barkhouse of Bridgewater, Nova Scotia, wrote that magazine article and has encouraged me to write too.

My first husband, Michael Wood of Oakville, Ontario, travelled with me to Nova Scotia and helped with my research. My second husband, Dave Adeney of Burlington, Ontario, also travelled with me to Nova Scotia, as well as France and Jersey, British Channel Islands, helped with my research, and invested many hours in editing my work.

Barry Cahill, a senior archivist at the Nova Scotia Archives and Records Management in Halifax, has tirelessly answered questions and given invaluable suggestions. Margaret Conrad, history professor at Acadia University in Wolfville, Nova Scotia, sent encouraging e-mail. The late gentleman, author, and historian John V. Duncanson squired me around his town of Falmouth, Nova Scotia, on three occasions and encouraged me in my research. Eleanor James, chief executive officer of the Oakville Public Library, granted me a six-month leave of absence to pursue my dream of writing about Marie Anne and Louis. Joan Payzant of Dartmouth, Nova Scotia, has been very supportive of this project. The late Esther Clark Wright of Wolfville, Nova Scotia, gave advice and encouragement. Anne Osselin of Rouen, France, has done research in Caen and Paris and transcribed pages of eighteenth-century handwriting. Librarian Angela Max, and genealogical researcher Jack Worrall, both of the Société Jersiaise in St. Helier, Jersey, Channel Islands, were most helpful. Translators Christine Pintar of Toronto and Janine Tortell of Oakville, Ontario, transformed French text into invaluable information in English and communicated my letters to France.

Publisher Dorothy Blythe, and editor Sandra McIntyre, of Nimbus Publishing in Halifax took a chance on a new author.

I hope my fellow Payzant descendants will enjoy reading about our progenitors Marie Anne and Louis, and appreciate their move to our country. May my sons, David and Andrew Wood of Toronto, Ontario, finally understand what my obsession has been all about: documenting the exciting lives of one of their sixty-four sets of fifth great-grandparents.

the owner of the *Mary* was not Louis Payzant, but Philip Dumaresq (a possible relative of court writer Jean Dumaresq, the St. Helier godfather of two of Louis' sons).

The list of ships states that the *Mary* was a "French Prize Condemned at London in 1747."[34] That meant that it was a French ship captured during the War of the Austrian Succession (which took place between 1740 and 1748 and involved Britain and France). The *Mary* would have been captured by a privateer licensed by the British government to seize enemy ships and their cargo. Taken to London in 1747, the *Mary* was sold at a public auction, the captor receiving up to half the amount obtained, and the government receiving the rest. Six years later, on May 22, 1753, in Jersey, the *Mary* was registered to Dumaresq, possibly indicating a sale by Louis just prior to his departure from St. Helier.

This two-masted square-rigged ship was captained by Peter St. Croix, who led a five-man crew. There were nine passengers: Louis and Marie Anne Payzant, their children (who by this time were aged six, five, three, and two), and servants Anne and Jacques Riovant, and Charles Langlois, possibly a relative of Louis. The *Mary*'s hold carried fabric and clothing: eighty dozen pairs of hose (likely from Jersey), twelve night waistcoats, woolen stuff (perhaps bolts of fabric), twenty pairs of blankets (sold in pairs), and "38 pair Men & Womens shoes British Manufacture." This cargo did not belong to Louis, but may have been sold to Dumaresq by him.

After success in France, and again in Jersey, Louis was headed for another challenge, though one much farther away and under much different circumstances. Crossing the Atlantic took perhaps six weeks, leaving ample time for Louis and Marie Anne to ponder what lay ahead of them. Little did they know that as Britain and France moved into the Seven Years' War, they would face unspeakable horrors of their own.

CHAPTER THREE

Lunenburg, a New Beginning
(1753–1756)

I n July 1753, the *Mary's* passengers and crew were relieved to set foot on dry land in Halifax after the Atlantic voyage. They knew it would take days to shake off their sea legs after weeks of nothing to look at but the rising and falling horizon. The children practically leaped down the gangway, excited to be in a new country. What they were really dying to see, though, were the "Indians." In Nova Scotia, it was the Mi'kmaq they would have heard stories about—some untrue, some true.

Stretching their legs by walking around Halifax, the four-year-old capital of Nova Scotia, they saw a fenced settlement cleared from the woods. It was a busy town, from the ships unloading at the docks to the soldiers on the parade and children running down the hills. Five rows of assorted buildings ran up the slope on the west side of the harbour, all surrounded by a ten-foot-high palisade with five blockhouses to protect it from the Mi'kmaq. For the settlers' enlightenment, St. Paul's Church, topped with a spire, sat on the central square, and for their punishment, the stocks and gallows waited at the water's edge.

Halifax was founded in 1749 to give Britain a larger presence in Nova Scotia. By the terms of the Treaty of Utrecht in 1713, France ceded to Britain "all Nova Scotia or Acadia according to its ancient boundaries,"[1] while retaining for itself the islands of Île Royale (Cape Breton) and Île Saint Jean (Prince Edward Island). In 1717 France began work on the Fortress of Louisbourg on Cape Breton, which took several decades to complete. (Since its costs were so great, King Louis XV apparently remarked that he expected to get up from his royal bed one morning to see the fortress' ramparts rising on the horizon.)

Although the British captured the fortress in 1744, they had to return it to the French four years later by the Treaty of Aix-la-Chapelle. Britain then needed to counterbalance the renewed French military strength to protect the shipping routes between Britain and the Thirteen Colonies.

Nova Scotia's new governor was London-born Edward Cornwallis, son of Baron Cornwallis, and identical twin of the Archbishop of Canterbury. Edward Cornwallis retired from the military in 1748 at the age of thirty-five. A lieutenant-colonel, he had served seventeen years in the British Army.[2] The next year the Board of Trade appointed him commander and first governor of the settlement of Chebucto (*Chebookt* in Mi'kmaq, meaning "chief harbour") in Nova Scotia. Chebucto was later re-named Halifax in honour of George Montagu-Dunk, the Earl of Halifax and chief of the Board of Trade. In the summer of 1749, Colonel Cornwallis sailed from London bound for the new land with 2,576 mainly cockney Londoners who had responded to advertisements in the *London Gazette*.

After landing in Halifax, Cornwallis wrote to the English secretary of state, the Duke of Bedford, describing the settlement: "From the Shore to the top of the Hill is about half a mile, the ascent very gentle, the Soil is good, there is convenient landing for Boats all along the Beach."[3] On July 2, 1749, he wrote to Lord Halifax, his disappointment apparent, "The number of settlers, men, women and children [actually the total of adult males] is 1400, but I beg leave to observe to your Lordships that amongst these the number of industrious active men proper to undertake and carry on a new settlement is very small....The rest are poor idle worthless vagabonds that embraced the opportunity to get provisions for one year without labour, or sailors that only wanted a passage to New England."[4]

His request for more settlers, Swiss and German Protestants in particular, was granted. The Board of Trade had agreed to send to Nova Scotia no more than fifteen hundred Foreign Protestants with the following conditions:

> [They must be]...willing to become loyal subjects of this Britannic Majesty [who] would receive in Nova Scotia each a grant of fifty acres of land, free of quit-rents and taxes for ten years, and thereafter not more than one shilling per annum for any fifty acres so granted. For every dependent woman or child there would be given an additional ten acres, and further grants would be made on the like conditions...as their families shall increase, or in Proportion to their abilities to cultivate the same. Immigrants

would receive free subsistence for twelve months from the date of their arrival in Nova Scotia. They shall be furnished with Arms and Ammunition as far as will be judged necessary, with a proper Quantity of Materials and Utensils for Husbandry [axes, saws, hoes, ploughs], clearing and cultivating their Lands, erecting Habitations, carrying on the Fishery, and such other Purposes as shall be necessary for their Support.[5]

The new settlers arrived between 1750 and 1752, around which time Cornwallis resigned. He returned to London in 1752, and was replaced by the English military officer Colonel Peregrine Thomas Hopson, who was about sixty-five years old and had at one time been governor of Fortress Louisbourg.

By 1753, Halifax was progressing well. The Church of England's St. Paul's Church had been erected in the summer of 1750, using timbers shipped from Boston. The *Halifax Gazette* had set up its printing presses in March 1752, the first in Canada. Wharves were built for the busy harbour.

Governor Hopson was determined to relocate Halifax's unhappy German- and French-speaking Protestants. Some had waited two to three years for their promised free farm lots, but the government hesitated due to the danger of attacks by the allied Acadians and Mi'kmaq. Hopson obtained supplies from the British government and chose a site south of Halifax for the new colony at Merligash ("Milky Bay," a Mi'kmaw name first mentioned in British records in 1630[6]). In May 1753, Hopson re-named the site Lunenburg (after one of King George II's German titles[7]), and appointed Lieutenant-Colonel Charles Lawrence and Captain Patrick Sutherland to be in charge of the new settlement. From Halifax, the first of two lots of settlers, baggage, workmen, building materials, and provisions sailed in a flotilla of fourteen ships for Lunenburg early in the morning of May 29.

Poor weather turned the usual one-day easy sail to Lunenburg into a ten-day ordeal, with the flotilla forced to anchor for a week behind the shelter of Mauger's Beach, not even past Cape Sambro. Weather wasn't the only problem. Overcrowding on the last three vessels required the shuffling of passengers to other ships. Three children were found whose parents were back in Halifax—they were returned home. Rations were exhausted, so twenty-eight more casks were sent from Halifax. A baby was born and one of the surgeons on board reported that mother and child were both fine. Conditions must have been vile at times: orders were sent to the captains to allow the passengers on deck so the "Vessels' holds might be cleaned and sweetened in the mean time."[8] No doubt these already disgruntled settlers —future neighbours of Louis and Marie Anne—were frustrated with the delay.

In Halifax in July 1753, Louis Payzant probably sought out Governor Hopson to personally deliver the letter of recommendation from John Pownall, secretary to the Board of Trade in London, and to find out just where he and his family could settle. On July 30, ten days after Louis had arrived, the governor's secretary wrote to Pownall: "His Excelly [Excellency] received your favour of the 26th April, concerning Mr. Lewis Payzant and his Family who he has sent to the New Settlement of Lunenburg, there to be on the same footing with the Foreign Settlers."[9] Though Halifax would have been a natural location for a merchant or agent, perhaps the governor encouraged Louis to set up business in Lunenburg, and be a help to the French-speaking group already there. Besides, there was good farm land in Lunenburg that could support Louis' future business during lean times.

On August 6, 1753, the *Mary* departed Halifax for Newfoundland, which was more important commercially at that time than Nova Scotia due to its booming codfish industry. Its hold still contained the stockings, fabric, night waistcoats, blankets, and shoes from Jersey; "flower" and Nova Scotia rum had been added at Halifax.[10]

In the early 1750s, Newfoundland's fishing season population reached a peak of 16,000. The permanent population had grown to 5,000, including women and children, servants, agents, bookkeepers, clerks, carpenters, blacksmiths, sailmakers, etc. The total amount of exported salt codfish had exceeded 500,000 quintals (50,000 metric tons) three years earlier.[11]

Leaving Halifax near the end of July, the Payzants soon arrived at Lunenburg. From the harbour, they likely saw a hive of activity on the peninsula. A small army of 158 soldiers and 1,450 settlers were creating a new settlement on land that had been cleared a few years earlier by Acadians. In a pattern similar to Halifax's, running up the steep hill away from the narrow waterfront were six rows of assorted wooden huts or framed houses built in the knee-high grass, bushes, and small trees. Louis had no doubt been told in Halifax that the town plots were being surveyed and were now marked by numbered stakes in the ground.

The huts and houses were located in an orderly fashion on the settlers' lots, the numbers of which had been drawn earlier in Halifax. The adult men—those entitled to lots—had met in St. Paul's Church on Monday, May 21 at 7:00 A.M., at which time they each drew one card from a pack of playing cards marked with the lot numbers from the Lunenburg survey.[12]

Fortifications were already erected. To the west, Louis and Marie Anne would have noticed a fort already completed and a wooden palisade running up and over the hill. West of the palisade the land fell away sharply to a valley. East of the surveyed area stood a blockhouse on a hill. Beyond that, the peninsula stretched out to the sea. At the water's edge sat storehouses and a small wharf.

Observing the new settlement from the ship's deck, Marie Anne must have wondered why she ever consented to this move. At the age of forty-two, she no doubt missed the comforts of a stone home in the established and civilized town of St. Helier, Jersey. After rowing to the beach, Louis approached Lieutenant-Colonel Charles Lawrence for directions in obtaining his town and garden lots. Lawrence, a forty-four-year-old Londoner, was a popular military officer and relative of the Earl of Halifax. Tall, strong, and energetic, he had served in the army in Louisbourg, then in Halifax in 1752. At Hopson's request, Lawrence accompanied the settlers from Halifax to Lunenburg in June 1753.

After having met Louis and his family, Lawrence commented on them in a letter to Governor Hopson on August 8, 1753: "The Families from Jersey [the Payzants, the Riovant couple, and Charles Langlois] appear to be a contented, well disposed sort of people. I wish we had 500 such, to settle that fine harbour...and set an Example to the Germans of behaviour worthy of their imitation."[13]

Lawrence returned to Halifax in late August, leaving the settlement in the capable hands of Captain Patrick Sutherland. In May 1753, Sutherland had been appointed lieutenant-colonel of the Lunenburg militia regiment, justice of the peace, and chief magistrate for the township of Lunenburg. He remained in charge for about nine years after Lawrence's departure. Though a lieutenant-colonel, he was always referred to as "Colonel."[14]

Louis Payzant received a town lot for his house, a garden lot for vegetables, and a thirty-acre lot for firewood and grain crops. (Later, he was granted an island of one hundred acres and another of forty acres.) His town lot, E3 in Moreau's Division, measured forty by sixty feet. The six divisions, named after prominent leaders in the settlement, were used for administrative organization and the mustering of settlers in case of defense. Governor Hopson named the twelve streets after well-known British surnames (including his own). Louis' lot was on the north side of Townshend Street (after Charles Townshend, one of the lords in the Board of Trade), three lots east of

Third house from left on Townshend Street was location of Louis Payzant's town lot, 1753-1772. Lunenburg, Nova Scotia, 2002.

Duke Street. The whole block across the street was unoccupied, reserved for public or government space.

Louis probably hired local carpenters to build a frame house at the going labour rate of eighteen shillings a day. He would have used his allotted 500 bricks, 700 feet of boards, and 250 nails, and bought shingles, and frames for windows and doors, from New England ships. A month after the Payzants arrived, all the settlers had gardens, and many had "good Framed Houses."[15]

The townhouse may have resembled the earliest style, Cape Cod, which usually had between two and four low-ceilinged rooms on the ground floor, a sleeping loft in the half-storey upstairs, and a large central hearth for cooking and heating. Outside, the gable roof paralleled the harbour, the tops of the windows and doors met the overhanging eaves, and the exterior walls were clad in shingles or clapboard.

East of town, 570 garden lots of one quarter acre each were surveyed and ready for distribution in August of 1753. While that was too late in the season for planting, many settlers had started vegetable gardens on portions of their town lots as soon as they were ready in mid-June. Louis received his garden lot, F7, in the Third Division, north of the marsh near the bottom of the hill.

There were five hundred Lunenburg settlers capable of militia duty. Each of these able-bodied men and older boys was supplied with a musket to ward off raids. The local militia guards were headquartered at the fort on the eastern side—the "Eastern Blockhouse"—enclosed within a wall of pickets. For regular military protection, Lunenburg was served by ninety-two regular troops and sixty-six rangers from each of the three provincial regiments. They were housed in the barracks of the pentagon-shaped "Star Fort" built by the settlers at the top of the hill west of town.

Despite the building activity, all was not well. There were problems in Lunenburg and the settlers were disgruntled for several reasons. First, before the Germans had left their native lands, advertisements targeting these Foreign Protestants had incorrectly promised that the British government would supply free items: "necessary Furniture as Beds, Kettles, Pans, etc."[16] The immigrants sold their furniture before sailing to Nova Scotia and upon arrival discovered a shortfall. Second, some of the new immigrants were indebted to the British government for their passage and had to do public works labour—mostly construction jobs—as a form of payment. But this was hard to stomach for those who had lived in Halifax for a year or two before moving to Lunenburg and knew that the first settlers in 1749 had crossed the Atlantic free of charge.

The government tried to make amends. Because the settlers were disappointed with the tight food rations, the council in Halifax, with approval from London, increased the free provisions and extended them for several more years. Even so, these old grudges, plus new rumours and difficult personalities, served to incite an insurrection in the six-month-old town. In December 1753, an uprising put the garrison and militia to the test.

In late November and early December, rumours circulated about a letter received by twenty-nine-year-old town resident Jean Petrequin. It purportedly mentioned supplies that everyone should have received, but didn't—rice; butter; molasses; a pint of rum per person per day; shoes, stockings, shirts, and other clothing; £5 cash to cover the cost of their ocean crossing; and three shillings a day wages.

By mid-December 1753, Colonel Sutherland learned that a mob had seized Jean Petrequin and locked him in the Eastern Blockhouse. The mob demanded to see the letter that Petrequin claimed to have received from a relative—a high official in London. If the letter proved authentic, the locals would be furious over not receiving their promised items, believing that some government officials were keeping them for themselves. Tempers flared for several days, and at one point, two men were wounded.

Louis' house was only about four blocks from the Eastern Blockhouse where the mobs had swarmed. Historian Winthrop P. Bell writes: "Early on this Sunday morning the more active insurgents were summoning all settlers to assemble on the parade at nine o'clock, even threatening death to those who would not join them. Among these was...Louis Payzant, who either was, or professed to be, ill. Nevertheless the threats to burn his house over his head and kill his whole family seemed to him so serious that he had a friend take away his children, and he himself loaded his guns and prepared to defend himself if attacked."[17]

The family's fifteen quiet years in Jersey didn't prepare them for this, and they had only been in Nova Scotia six months—what were they getting themselves into? Marie Anne refused to leave Louis' side at this critical time and would have been thankful that a neighbour had taken the children for safekeeping. Louis, shaken and not really ill, wanted nothing to do with these rowdies who threatened him. He was sure they were jealous of his stature as a merchant and his friendship with Lawrence and Sutherland. Determined to protect his precious family, he had his musket ready.

Sutherland, realizing he couldn't contain the insurrection, sent an aide to Halifax for help. Two hundred soldiers commanded by Lieutenant-Colonel Robert Monckton arrived from Halifax, restored peace in the Eastern Blockhouse, and made sure all settlers had given up their arms. Listed on the Lunenburg Return of Arms, dated December 26–27, 1753, was Louis Payzant of Moreau's Division.

By mid-January of 1754, Monckton returned to Halifax, but left an officer and forty men to garrison the Eastern Blockhouse. In April in Halifax, a trial of the insurrectionists revealed that the illiterate Petrequin had been set up by John William Hoffman of Lunenburg. Hoffman, a known troublemaker, had held a grudge against Lunenburg civic leaders who had passed him over for the position of justice of the peace. The letter in fact never existed. Hoffman was sentenced to a £100 fine and two years in prison. He later moved to

Philadelphia where he made a fortune in the sugar trade. There were no more insurrections in Lunenburg.

After the trial, the pardoned insurgents and Jean Petrequin returned to Lunenburg. He and his wife Catherina were on the June 1755 victualling list (a record of names of those who received a free supply of food).

By the summer of 1754, most of the settlers had planted vegetables (potatoes and turnips) on their town lots, and oats, flax, and barley on the garden lots. The root vegetables, along with firewood, were shipped to Halifax for sale (Lunenburg was the main source of supply).

In September, the surveyors had finished marking the third set of lots (thirty-acre lots) promised by the government. Louis' was number four in Oakland. His narrow strip of land ran northeast from Mahone Harbour, almost opposite the present picturesque town of Mahone Bay. That same month, livestock from New England was shipped to Lunenburg: 847 sheep, 188 goats, 125 pigs, and 74 cows. Married men were paired to draw lots. Louis Payzant and Joseph Rous had to share ten sheep, three sows, and one goat. From another shipment in December of 145 sheep, 36 pigs, and a few chickens, Louis gained two more pigs and two more sheep. The fall of 1754 was extremely dry, yielding meager crops, and the winter of 1754–55 was severe. That spring, poor government planning led to a shortage of livestock feed, and as a result, a large number of animals died.

In June 1755, a list of 1,548 persons was compiled to show who had been victualled by the official Lunenburg storekeeper from his "wet" or "dry" stores in the warehouse at the water's edge. "Wet" referred to beef or pork stored in brine in tight-coopered casks from Ireland; "dry" referred to flour, hardtack (a saltless hard biscuit made from flour and water), rice, and dried peas from New England. On the victualling list were "Louis, Anna, Philip, Jeane, Louis Paysant & Maria Pasant; James, Jean, Anna Riovant, and Charles Langlois,"[18] as recorded by a German-speaking clerk. The Riovants now had a son, Jean.

Each person received per week seven pounds of bread (hardtack) and flour, one and three-quarter pounds of beef, two pounds of pork, one pint of "pease," and one-half pint of molasses. These rations were extended to March 1756, and again to June 1757, but without the meat, peas and molasses. The government hoped that by then the settlers would be more self-sufficient from their gardens and crops.

Lunenburg needed a Church of England minister, an essential position considering that the British government required its colonists to adhere to the Church of England as a gauge of political loyalty.

Protestant dissenters from the Church of England were allowed as settlers, but not papists.

Reverend Baptiste Moreau, aged about thirty-eight, was among the first wave of settlers to Lunenburg in early June 1753. A native of Dijon in France, he had been a Roman Catholic prior of an abbey near Brest in Brittany. Dissatisfied with the Catholic doctrines and practices, he left the church and emigrated to England. There, he married, and after being hired as a missionary with an annual salary of £70, left in June 1749 with Cornwallis for Nova Scotia.

The SPG (the British "Society for the Propagation of the Gospel in Foreign Parts") was Moreau's employer. An auxiliary of the Church of England, it provided salaries for its missionaries in new settlements until parish tithes could be raised to support them. For Moreau, it also supplied French prayer books.

After three years as assistant minister in Halifax, Moreau accepted the position of Anglican minister in Lunenburg. One week after arriving there in June 1753 with his wife, young children, and servants, he preached an open-air Sunday service in French, German, and English, although his command of the latter two languages was weak. The group of French-speaking settlers from Montbéliard (now in southeast France, but then a principality between France and Switzerland) were Lutherans who easily adapted to the Anglican Church. For eight years Moreau was the only ordained clergyman in Lunenburg.

By the fall of 1754, Moreau had his church, St. John's, under construction. Measuring forty by sixty feet, it was built from wood imported from Boston (local sawmills had not yet been established). Politics between Halifax and London slowed funding down, so St. John's was not fully completed for another nine years. Thankful for a French-speaking minister, Louis and Anne Marie attended Moreau's services. Since their town lot was almost kitty-corner to St. John's, they would have observed its construction.

In October 1754, the local schoolmaster reported a fairly constant attendance of sixty French-speaking children of all ages. Moreau appointed George Frederick Bailly on behalf of the SPG, which paid for the position. The curriculum included reading and writing, singing psalms, and learning catechism. Since Bailly held classes in his own house, just three blocks from the Payzant home, he taught Philip, Mary, and John, though not three-year-old Lewis. The six-month school term ran from the beginning of November to the end of April. Children had to help out on the country lots during the summer, and Bailly also had to work his own land to help support his young family.

Lawrence wanted merchants to set up businesses in Lunenburg. In a letter to Hopson that first summer of 1753, Lawrence wished he could attract merchants in "Shiptimber, boat-building, barrel-staves and hoops, boards and planks and the fishery"[19] so that settlers could be employed and earn income to buy items not supplied by the government. He wrote about how good it would be to have "some such among us whose substance and knowledge in trade might find imployment for the poorer sort of the people."[20]

One of the first merchants was Captain Joseph Rous, who, likely in the fall of 1753, began to catch fish in Lunenburg, and salt-cure them in casks for export. Months earlier in May in Halifax, he had been appointed "Director of Transports and Inspector of the Lumber,"[21] the supervisor of the government-issued building supplies in Lunenburg. This New Englander had moved to Lunenburg from Halifax with his family, and later owned Rous Island, just north of Payzant's Island.

During the first winter, some settlers made staves and barrel hoops, possibly for Rous' fishing business. Most of the Germans had been farmers, and were not much interested in fishing. Not for several generations would fishing become an important industry in Lunenburg.

Some merchants must have already set up businesses in Lunenburg, because in January 1754 several of them ordered supplies from Webb & Ewer in Halifax, and that year a Cape Sable Indian chief paid off some debts owed to Lunenburg merchants. Lawrence wrote to Sutherland expressing his eagerness to encourage more business enterprises. It is unknown what Louis did during those years in Lunenburg—he could have been a merchant or commission agent. It is known, however, that he had boxes and bales of English goods that he purchased in Halifax or Boston.

Louis was granted number seven in the "Islands of Mahone Bay,"[22] and a smaller one southeast of it,[23] both north of Lunenburg. The turmoil of the insurrection in town months earlier made island life seem attractive. Louis and Anne Marie would feel safer being away from the rebellious Germans, and they could pasture their livestock without fencing or having to pay someone to tend them in a common field. The island soil was known to be good. Thus Louis arranged for the construction of a temporary island dwelling that would house his family plus the three Riovants and Charles Langlois for the winter of 1755. A better home could be built later. They all looked forward to the peace of their island sanctuary.

CHAPTER FOUR

Island Attack
(1756)

Fifty-nine-year-old Louis felt alive on his island—here, he was king of his own domain. Marie Anne wasn't too keen yet, but she'd warm to it—at least she was away from the grumbling settlers in Lunenburg. And she had good reason to be a little out of sorts these days—she was pregnant. The news thrilled Louis, as this would be their child of the new world.

Marie Anne was a loving wife and mother, and the children were flourishing. The boys and their sister delighted in roaming all over the island—to the north hill, the large lake, and the south hill where their new house was under construction. They had never seen deer, beaver, or so many different birds before. It was wonderful to drift off to sleep lulled by the waves lapping on the island's stony beaches.

The Crown granted Louis Payzant this island (known as Payzant's Island[1]), and a smaller one, likely in 1754. While settlers regarded the islands as desirable, Lieutenant-Governor Lawrence hesitated to let them get into the hands of "ordinary" settlers. He gave greater consideration to applications from "gentlemen" who met strict conditions—this may have been how Louis received his.[2]

In the spring of 1756, when the recently sown field of wheat was green,[3] Louis' two-storey frame house was being built while the family lived next to it in a simple log cabin. He employed local soldiers stationed at the Lunenburg fort to build the house.

Louis planned to carry on a trade from his island. His packaged English merchandise was stored in the log cabin, no doubt cramping the living quarters. His intention was probably to use these items as the nucleus of a dry goods business, with which, as a good

Huguenot, he hoped to become very successful.

> "[Louis]...settled on one of the Island[s] in Mahone Bay...Where he had a great prospect of in larging himself by commerce: and While he was promising himself Great things in the world; The providance of God was contriving a way to cut of[f] his expectation. Oh How little are men acqua[i]nted with the ways of God."[4]

But the next event in Louis Payzant's life would prevent that outcome from even becoming a reality.

Though only seven at the time, John remembered every detail of what happened next. It changed his life forever, along with the lives of his mother and brothers and sister.

On Thursday evening, May 8, 1756, all the men who had been working on the house, as well as Charles Langlois and Jacques Riovant, left the island. Louis kept his musket handy to defend himself and his family from any disgruntled Germans in the area—the authorities had advised him to open fire if they were disturbed. An Indian attack was a remote possibility, too. Just seven years old at the time, son John would never forget the events of that night:

> Abote midnight there came ten Indian[s] from the River St. John (now new-Brunswick) and the Island on which we were at that time was destitute of men which I suppose was the only time since it had been settled. [At] midnight the Dogs made an unusel noise, which alarmed my Father. He got up and armed himself, opened the door and made a discharge only with powder, not knowing who they were, three of them took aim at his flash and killed him on the spote, then they plundered the House, which was full of English Goods, of which they took as much as they thought fit, then they Killed a man that they had took on their way for a pilot [a young guide from Rous Island], and likeways a servant woman with her Child of two years old [Anne and Jean Riovant]. The woman['s] Husband [Jacques Riovant] a few days before had run away and saved his life. So that there was no man on the Island but my Father and him Dead at the door.[5]

Another son, Lewis, adds to the unpleasant memory the following, from an interview:

> Supposing that some of those malcontents were now about the house, [Louis] seized his musket, and went out to oppose them. Imagining, no doubt, a slight demonstration in the "line of battle," would frighten them, he discharged his piece. Alas! he had mistaken

the danger that threatened him, and the mistake was fatal! The harmless flash of his gun revealed his position. It was answered by a volley from the assailants. The terrified wife and mother rushed out just in time to throw her arms around her fainting husband. She begged him to come in. Death choked his utterance as he exclaimed, "my heart is growing cold!—the Indians!" and he fell lifeless at her feet. The terrific 'war-whoop,' and the rush of the Indians confirmed her worst forebodings. Resistance was out of the question....They rushed in like so many tigers.[6]

One of the warriors raced to Louis' body. As was the practice, he braced his knee against Louis' shoulders and ripped the scalp off the skull from the nape of the neck to the front.[7] The scalp would be a trophy (for a reward) and proof of the attacker's prowess.

Brandishing the dripping scalp, he cried out in the frenzy of the moment, then fastened the scalp to a belt that held others.

The raiding party had first landed on Rous Island (just north of Payzant's), which was occupied by a tenant family. They killed an Irish man, then tied his son's hands behind his back and forced him to guide them to Payzant's Island. Once they arrived, the Indians killed and scalped the son. When his body was found three days later, his hands were still tied behind his back.[8]

The barbaric act of scalping was not new in 1756. Records indicate that in North America native tribes scalped enemies in the sixteenth century. In 1535 Jacques Cartier described how Indians dried and stretched scalps of their enemies. In 1609 Samuel de Champlain wrote of Indian scalps hung on sticks.[9]

Many journals describe acts of scalping from the Seven Years' War (1756–1763), some indicating that a few souls even survived. In May 1756 at Oswego, New York, French-allied Indians scalped a very drunken British soldier and left him for dead. Miraculously, he recovered.[10]

The warring French and British in North America revived the act of scalping (their soldiers scalped Indians, too), and promised bounties to their respective Indian allies as proof of enemies slain. Entrepreneurial natives created scalps from horsehair, or even divided one human scalp into three. At the discovery of this ruse, the authorities examined scalps more carefully.[11]

On Payzant's Island, Marie Anne dashed back into the house to bar the door while the natives howled their war-whoops. But her efforts were useless—the attackers entered by force. Suddenly head of the family, nine-year-old Philip sprang to the table shaking his fists at the intruders, trying his best to defend his terrified mother, sister Mary, and little brothers John and Lewis.[12]

Some of the natives grabbed the boxes of merchandise and tossed them outside to be loaded into the canoes. They may have had previous information concerning Louis' stock of merchandise stored on the island—making Louis' island an enticing target.

The natives torched both the log cabin and the new one, then they took the trembling Marie Anne and the whimpering children down to the canoes and pushed off into the night. The fire began as a crackle and grew to engulf both wooden dwellings. The flames roared higher and higher. The ceiling beams collapsed, shooting out a shower of bright cinders. For several days the charred remains whistled and hissed. Areas of glowing embers suddenly turned orange from gusts of wind, then burned out and turned to charcoal.

The bodies of Anne Riovant and her son were found near the water. Perhaps she had snatched the child from his bed and stumbled down to the beach, at which point an Indian seized the shrieking boy by the feet and "dashed out the brains of the babe"[13] against a rock or tree trunk. (This was not an uncommon way to kill children at the time. In a 1690 massacre of sixty by French and Iroquois at Schenectady, New York, children's heads "were smashed against doors and windows."[14] In 1704, Indians smashed out the brains of a newborn against a doorpost.[15])

Why did the natives spare Marie Anne and her children? Ransom was greater for a live prisoner than a scalp, and these Indians wanted a reward for their hard work. The payment at that time for a British scalp was 100 livres.[16] Also, they might have been shocked to hear Marie Anne speak French, the language of their employers, the Quebec officer Charles Boishébert, and the Jesuit missionary Charles Germain. Perhaps the Indians thought Marie was Acadian.

But if that was the case, why did they kill the other five people in Mahone Bay? Louis was no doubt shot because he was armed and would have fired back if they had missed. The guide's father possibly put up resistance, too. I can only assume that Anne Riovant, her son, and the young guide were all killed in the heat of the moment.

Marie Anne and her family were war victims caught in the clash between her native France and the British government of the colony she lived in. Just ten days after the attack on Payzant's Island, Britain formally declared war on France, beginning the international conflict history knows as the Seven Years' War. Tragically, civilian deaths are a part of war.

The Indians who raided Rous and Payzant's Islands were not the local Nova Scotia Mi'kmaq (who had grievances against the British and were allied with the French), but Maliseet from Sainte Anne's Jesuit Mission (near present-day Fredericton, New Brunswick) in what was then called Acadia, an area of French-speaking Roman Catholics.

The Maliseet are part of the Eastern Algonquin nations. Their territory stretched northwest from the Bay of Fundy, following the Saint John River to the Saint Lawrence River, and included the northern part of the state of present-day Maine. This area was part of Acadia, claimed by both the British and French. By law (the 1713 Treaty of Utrecht) it was a British possession, but, in fact, it was occupied by Acadians (at least those who had evaded the Expulsion in 1755) and protected by Quebec.

The Roman Catholic mission of Sainte Anne's, where the Maliseet raiding party had originated, was run by Jesuits. This religious order of men, founded in Paris in 1534 and also called the Society of Jesus, arrived in New France around 1630. Their primary mission was to educate and convert the natives from their "heathen ways" to Roman Catholicism. In Acadia the missionaries were to convert the Maliseet and Mi'kmaq and aid the French authorities by inciting the Indians to raid British territory.

The priests instilled in the Maliseet an absolute hatred for the heretical Protestant *Bastonnais*, which provided great zeal in their raids.[17] The French term *Bastonnais* literally meant the "Bostonians," but to the Maliseet it meant simply the enemy: any Protestant from New England, or Old England, it didn't matter. Maliseet used the term to frighten their children, equating *Bastonnais* with the bogeyman.[18]

To the French authorities, the raids on British territory were part of a larger plan. The Marquis de la Jonquière, governor of New France from 1749–1752, wrote: "It is desirable that the Savages [a term used by the French colonial authorities to describe all the native tribes in New France] succeed in destroying the plans of the English as well as their establishment in Halifax. It is up to the missionaries to negotiate with the Savages and to direct their actions. Reverend Father German [Germain]...will have no difficulty making the best use of them."[19] The atrocities carried out during Indian raids were very important to the French, wrote the next governor general, Vaudreuil, on June 8, 1756, because "there is no surer way to sicken the people of the English colonies of war and to make them desire the return of peace."[20]

In New France, the French allied with Algonquin nations in raids against the British, who in turn, allied with Iroquoian nations. In Acadia, the French rewarded the Maliseet for prisoners and scalps with money, rum, brandy, finished clothing (shirts, coats, stockings, shoes), beads, copperware and other household utensils, kettles, knives, axes, gimlets, hatchets, guns and gunpowder, tobacco and smoking pipes.[21]

In Nova Scotia and Acadia, the Maliseet, Mi'kmaq, Acadians, and British settlers were all pawns caught in the hostilities of the Seven Years' War of 1756–1763. This first global war pitted Britain (with its allies Prussia and Hanover) against France (along with Austria, Sweden, Saxony, Russia, and Spain). Britain aimed to eliminate France as a commercial rival by destroying its navy and merchant fleet, and seizing its colonies, where most of the battles took place.[22]

The original plan for the Nova Scotia raids came from Quebec. There, in 1756, Pierre de Vaudreuil de Cavagnial, Marquis de Vaudreuil, fifty-eight-year-old governor general of New France, wrote to his superior, the minister of the marine in Versailles, that he had ordered a Quebec officer to attack the British in various locations. (That officer was Boishébert, who, obeying orders, sent a detachment of Maliseet to Lunenburg.) Vaudreuil's goals: to forestall anticipated British attacks; to prevent the British from interrupting the return of the Acadians, who had been brutally ousted by them a year earlier; and to protect those Acadians who had managed to remain.[23]

One of the objects of the French attack, the raid of May 8 on Payzant's Island, was described by twenty-six-year-old Dettlieb Christopher Jessen, deputy provost marshall in Lunenburg.[24] On May 11, he wrote:

> This day we have received Intellidgend in Town that Last
> Thursday the 8 day of May the Indians were fallen in at Mahone
> Bay upon Louis Paysants Island where the[y] have kild him & his
> maid Servant and her Child, & have Carried his wife & four
> Children herlong with them, & Likewise the Indian[s] have kild
> the Same day at Capt. Rouse Island an old man & a Growing Son
> of Him. whereof Colonell Sutherland has Dispatched a Command
> of about thirty Man with the Officers in Order to visit the Said
> Island, the[y] found that it was So, & Likewise the house was
> bournd down to the Ground & all their Effects where Gan [were
> gone].[25]

In Lunenburg on May 12, Colonel Sutherland sent a dispatch to Lieutenant-Governor Lawrence in Halifax. "Yesterday in the afternoon," he began, "I received the melancholly account of Mr. Pizant's House being burned (in Mahone Bay) and that himself and other people were killed. I immediately sent an officers party which returned this morning by whom I am informed that on Pizants Island the House is burned, he with another young man kill'd near it and scalp'd. A woman Servant and Child also kill'd and scalp'd near the water side. His wife and four Children missing."[26]

Lieutenant-Governor Lawrence received the dispatch from Lunenburg with its shocking news about Payzant, who Lawrence had remembered favourably from the summer of 1753. As acting governor (he officially became governor a few months later), he immediately called a council meeting with six members in attendance. They reviewed letters about recent Indian raids: one on April 26 and 27 on the Chignecto Isthmus (at the border of present-day Nova Scotia and New Brunswick) in which nine men were killed and scalped, and the May 8 raid on Rous and Payzant's Islands.

The council advised Lawrence to defend the British forts from the French-incited Indian raids by raising two hundred men from the New England troops at Chignecto, and to increase the bounty paid by the province for captured Indians or their scalps. A proclamation dated May 14 reads in part: "the Indians have of late, in a most treacherous and cruel Manner, killed and carried away divers of his Majesty's Subjects in different Parts of the Province."[27] The new bounty was £30 for each live Indian male over the age of sixteen, and £25 for the scalp of the same, and also for each live Indian woman or child.

In 1756 the bodies of Louis, Anne and Jean, and the young guide and his father were not taken into Lunenburg for burial. There is no mention of their names for that year in the burial records of St. John's Church in Lunenburg.[28] Perhaps the soldiers just buried them on the site.

Nova Scotia folklorist Helen Creighton thought differently. Referring to Louis, she wrote in 1950: "They say on Heckman's Island [a large island east of Lunenburg] that the body was taken there for burial in a grove of trees, and that the grass beside the tree where he lies has always been green and remains green to this day. Some people also claim to have heard supernatural sounds."[29]

A remarkable version of the Payzant scalping was written by the French three months afterwards. On August 6, 1756, Governor General Vaudreuil reported to France on the state of Acadian affairs, boasting of the raid on Payzant's Island. However, his statement had either been greatly embellished, or he himself had been misinformed:

> A detachment of Indians that this officer [Boishébert] sent to
> Merligueche [Lunenburg] killed on the island 20 inhabitants,
> burned two large warehouses, took a woman and three of her chil-
> dren. This woman has said she was a native of Caen in Normandy,
> that she was there for two years on this island and that there were

many French who inhabited this island against their will. It is unfortunate that the Indian attacks were directly aimed at these French, especially if they are not there of their own free will at Merligueche. I am writing to Mr. Boishébert to learn from this woman if it would not be possible to incite the French to a revolt. I am making him aware that this attempt [revolt] requires much caution. It would be preferable that these French could stage a memorable surprise attack, like the burning of Merligueche and then quickly move off to our land. [30]

An account written almost a hundred years after the Payzant raid is chillingly vivid because it was based on an interview with a witness. The author was forty-two-year-old Silas Tertius Rand, a Nova Scotia Baptist minister, missionary to the Mi'kmaq, philologist, and ethnologist, whose brothers-in-law were descended from Louis and Marie Anne Payzant. Rand interviewed Lewis, the last remaining Payzant child, who died in 1845 at the then-remarkable age of ninety-four. He had been five when his father was scalped.

> Nearly a century had passed away when Mr. Payzant told us the story. He was literally bending under the weight of years. Both mind and body were enfeebled by age. It was some time before we could get him fully roused. But he well remembered the scene.
>
> As he dwelt upon it and related particular after particular, in answer to various enquiries, it came up more and more vividly to his recollection. We shall not easily forget the excitement of his manner as he reverted, on one occasion, to the rush of the savages into the house when the door was opened. He drew up his bent and contracted form into an erect position. He raised his voice, and his eyes flashed. "O," said he, "I hear them now! I see them! Hewing down the boxes! Hewing down the boxes! Seizing and securing every valuable article as fast as they could!"
>
> He remembered too that his oldest brother gave battle....And he remembered how they [the Maliseet] afterwards mimicked her cries [his mother's] in their sports, and called out, as she had done, "Mr. Payzant, Mr. Payzant." And the old gentleman imitated, in turn, *their* voice and manner, as he related the story.[31]

Payzant's Island, now named Covey's Island, remained in the family for about fifty years. In 1761 Marie Anne had been given official permission to sell it (along with present-day Bachman's Island and a thirty-acre lot across from present-day Mahone Bay).[32] It wasn't until 1804, however, that her son Reverend John Payzant sold half the island to Adam Heckman for £10.[33] What happened to the other half is unknown.

Several people lived on the island after Louis. In 1870, historian Mather Byles DesBrisay recorded: "After the members of the Payzant family, whose lives had been spared, were carried off, a man named Covey lived on the island. He was followed in succession by Adam Heckman, Paul Langille, Peter Herman, and Casper Meisner."[34] Perhaps the "Covey" was a descendant of Charles Covey, who lived in Halifax that first year of 1749. Still called "Covey's Island" in 1864, the name was officially approved on July 15, 1936.[35] The Payzant story will be forever connected to the island, despite its present designation.

CHAPTER FIVE

Maliseet Trek
(1756)

Marie Anne sat in stunned silence as the Maliseet quickly, silently, and powerfully propelled their canoes carrying her and the children into the night. Where were these murderers taking them? Would their lives be spared? She worried that her captors might soon turn their violence on her and rip off her scalp, adding it to Louis'—she couldn't bear to look at it—now hanging from the belt of the sweating monster in front of her. Who would look after the children then? She was completely at the mercy of the Indians—an escape back to Lunenburg and safety would be impossible. She silently prayed for strength and guidance. It was all she could do.

On their hasty retreat into the darkness from Payzant's Island, the Maliseet captors travelled from the British-occupied south shore of Nova Scotia to the French-occupied Acadian area near the Minas Basin. They probably canoed across Mahone Bay north to East River and up long, skinny Panuke Lake, which empties via St. Croix River into the Minas Basin.

By morning they would have passed below Fort Edward. Marie Anne might have seen a speck of red—a British soldier on guard up

Maliseet birchbark canoe.

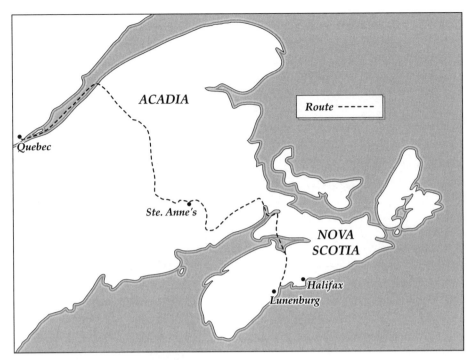

Map of Maliseet trek to Quebec.

there—and wondered how to get his attention. However, the Maliseet had threatened her and the children with tomahawks, warning them to keep completely silent.[1] "They were all ordered to lie flat in the canoes and taken down at low water hugging the high bank of the flat towards the fort and passing under its banks."[2] Any opportunity to escape or attract the soldier's attention would have meant certain death for her or one of her children—or for them all.

Fort Edward, named for Governor Edward Cornwallis, had been erected in 1750 to protect the British overland route from Halifax to the Bay of Fundy via the Minas Basin. Pisiquid (Mi'kmaq for "junction of waters," or "flowing square into the sea"[3]), the area around the fort, had been populated by Acadians since 1685.[4] Fort Edward provided a strong British presence in the area to deter Acadians from using their overland commercial routes to other French settlements in the Chignecto area or to Louisbourg on Cape Breton.

Acadia, first governed by France, came under British rule after the 1713 Treaty of Utrecht. At that time the nearly two thousand Acadians proclaimed themselves "neutral French," claiming allegiance to nei-

"View of Fort Edward in Piziguit River, Nova Scotia, 1753" by John Hamilton (now Windsor, Nova Scotia).

ther France nor England. In 1755 the lieutenant-governor of Nova Scotia, Charles Lawrence, frustrated over the refusal of the Acadians to swear allegiance to the British Crown, and pressured by Massachusetts and Britain, decided with his council to send the Acadians into exile. For the next eight years, over three-quarters of the Acadian population (by then ten thousand men, women, and children) were deported, mainly to New England. The French call it *Le Grand Dérangement* (The Great Upheaval); the English refer to it as the Expulsion.

It was at Fort Edward in 1755 that the local Pisiquid Acadians had been told they would be expelled from Nova Scotia because they refused to pledge allegiance to the British Crown. The fort's commanding officer, Captain Alexander Murray, ordered all 183 male Acadians aged ten and over in the Pisiquid area to report to the fort. There he announced that their land and cattle had been forfeited to the Crown and that they and their families would be removed from the province.[5] In October, about one thousand Acadians from Pisiquid were placed on four ships bound for New England. The next spring, as Marie Anne passed the fort, it no doubt held some Acadian prisoners captured after they had fled to the woods the previous fall.

The journey through the wilderness with the Maliseet must have seemed endless to Marie Anne. But one moment would have been seared into her memory. She spied a Maliseet holding up her wedding shoes, the sun glinting off the silver fabric. He had opened one of the looted packages—the precious merchandise that had represented Marie Anne and Louis' financial start in the new country, a dream now shattered. Memories of her happy wedding sixteen years earlier, an ocean away, flooded over her, temporarily obliterating her constant fear of the unknown. She instinctively reached out and asked to keep them, but the Maliseet simply laughed and tossed them over the gunwales.[6] She probably longed to disappear like that, too, but her children needed her now, especially the one in her belly, a last reminder of Louis.

Her captors were fierce warriors. They smeared their faces with red and black stripes[7] and protected their legs and feet with leather leggings and moccasins. These Maliseet warriors were also expert canoeists, who could travel 110 kilometres daily without fatigue. Marie Anne was no doubt completely intimidated by these strange men who had been so violent on Payzant's Island, yet who did not molest her. (Though they were often brutal during raids, most warriors respected their female captives.)[8]

The light birchbark canoes carried a paddle, gun, hatchet, blanket, and cooking vessel, as well as the plundered English goods. During portages, these supplies were wrapped in blankets and carried as a backpack, braced by a strap worn around the forehead. Marie Anne must have marvelled at the Maliseets' endurance and ability to be completely at home in the wild, something to which she was totally foreign.

A Maliseet became master of the person he had captured; only he was eligible for the reward on return to the French for a healthy captive. The captive's former identity was considered "dead," and the captive had to submit to the captor. A captive could be reborn when adopted into the tribe as a slave or replacement of a dead Maliseet.[9]

The youngest child Lewis, only five years old, "fell into the hands of a cruel master, who often during the canoe passage afterwards would throw him ashore by the hair of his head."[10] Yet en route this Maliseet had picked up his wife and young son, and during the journey he carried the two boys alternately on his back. "He would take me," said Lewis, "by the shoulders and swing me round upon his back."[11] These Maliseet were completely unpredictable: one minute brutal, the next, considerate.

For the first few days of the journey, a rapid retreat into French territory probably left little time for anyone to eat. Lewis later recalled his hunger: "sometimes they fed us upon berries; sometimes upon bread; and sometimes upon *nothing!*"[12]

Years later, one of Lewis' sons recalled his father telling him that during the journey, "The Indians came across two French men on a dyke [and] took their scalps to present for the reward saying that these scalps could not be distinguished from the English scalps and would bring as great a bounty."[13]

Following Indian trails, the group crossed the Minas Basin to present-day Parrsboro, then over the Chignecto Peninsula, partially by river, to the Cumberland Basin, and around to Shepody Bay. Leaving present-day Nova Scotia, they continued up the Petitcodiac River in what is today New Brunswick.

Once clear of enemy territory, the Maliseet prepared their scalp trophies. They scraped the flesh, dirt and dried blood from the skins and fashioned hoops of green wood over which each skin was stretched flat. After the scalps dried in the sun, the Maliseet painted the skins red, combed the hair, and fastened the finished trophies to the end of a long stick, which might hold up to fifteen dangling scalps.[14]

In 1757 (about a year after Marie Anne's capture), another prisoner recalled his stay at an encampment on the Petitcodiac River. Using tobacco juice as ink (according to legend), John Witherspoon kept a diary and hid it nightly. His master, he said, "took me to his house, and a poor cottage it is. A woman, a child, and a straw bed in it....The people here are kind of such as they have, but the style of husbandry carried on in this land is very bad, the spirit of industry they have not, they are an idle people running from house to house...pipes and tobacco is the chief of the business that is carried on in this place....Hear is a fine river...for fishen sammon, bearies, ...trout and what not. But the people are lazey, and lay up nothing for a rainy day."[15]

They had been travelling from Payzant's Island for about four days. As they paddled closer to their destination, a young warrior would have been sent ahead to announce the arrival of the party by shouting out how many warriors were lost, and how many scalps and prisoners were taken.[16] Marie Anne, no doubt exhausted, hungry, and still in shock, hoped this was the end of the arduous journey.

Both the Maliseet encampment of Aukpaque (Maliseet for "where the tide stops coming in") and the Acadian settlement of Sainte Anne's were very close to each other, about ten kilometres west of present-day Fredericton on the Saint John River.

Aukpaque, a summer campsite and burial ground, included present-day Savage and Harts Islands. It was probably inhabited seasonally, with a small permanent core population. Here, the Maliseet fished, gathered food from the forests, planted crops, settled their disputes, and allotted winter hunting grounds to each family. It was a place where the "Indians were accustomed to stop for a rest and a lightening of loads before tackling the hard climb up [upriver towards Quebec]. Ek-pa-hak, or Aukpaque, the head of tide, was one of their frequent camping places."[17]

In 1731, Acadian farmers, attracted by the excellent soil beside the river, founded Sainte Anne's. A few years later, the Jesuits opened a mission there. By 1756, when Marie Anne arrived, forty-nine-year-old Father Charles Germain had headed the mission for sixteen years. Born in Luxembourg, and educated as a Jesuit in Belgium and France, Germain was the liaison between the government of New France and the Maliseet under his guidance.[18]

Also at Sainte Anne's in 1756 was twenty-nine-year-old Captain Charles Deschamps de Boishébert of the colonial regular troops—the very officer who had carried out the orders for the Lunenburg raid that resulted in the murder of Louis Payzant.

Boishébert was born in Quebec to an army officer with Norman roots, and a mother whose father was Montreal's Governor Claude de Ramezay. Boishébert had served throughout New France from Acadia to present-day Detroit and Pennsylvania. An industrious, ingenious, determined officer, he had spent some time at court in Versailles.

Though he always returned to Quebec, Boishébert spent months at a time in Acadia carrying out the governor general's orders. To secure the Acadians' loyalty to France, this accomplished canoeist frequently travelled disguised as a habitant to visit the Acadians along the numerous bays and ports, often well into British territory. He studied the harbours between Acadia and Boston,[19] and moved as many Acadians back into the French area as he could. With the help of his Maliseet allies, he organized and participated in constant skirmishes against the British.

After the British expulsion of the Acadians in 1755, Boishébert was responsible for the resettlement and safety of those who had remained and those who eventually returned from exile in New England. Despite his efforts, there were times of extreme poverty due to a scarcity of supplies from Quebec.[20]

Aukpaque/Sainte Anne's was a diverse community when Marie Anne arrived there. Black-robed Jesuits at their mission tended to their flock of Maliseet and Acadians. Acadians farmed nearby but lived with their families at the settlement for protection. Acadian refugees, escapees from the British expulsion, lived here, too. French troops under command of Boishébert were stationed here. Maliseet men, women, and children camped on the nearby islands. British captives from other Maliseet raiding parties lived with the Indians. Food may have been at a premium for all, and it was too early in the season for new crops.

To celebrate the return of a successful Maliseet war party, a scalp dance was organized. Young women held up enemy scalps on poles while warriors danced around the fire to the beat of a drum, stamping, howling, and demonstrating how they had taken the scalps as proof of their valour. The Payzant children may have been taken to watch the spectacle. For these children, the realization that one of those scalps had been part of their father must have initiated such wild emotions that they might never have come to terms with them later in life.

The four children were adopted by the Maliseet to replace lost family members. At the adoption ceremony before the chief, his council, and the new families, the children were introduced by their new names. They were now considered full members of the clan. After the chief solemnly proclaimed their names, everyone cried out greetings of friendship. Release from adoption was difficult, if not impossible, as the Maliseet were accountable to no one in this matter.[21]

Lewis later recalled his time with the Maliseet. One night his master gave him a piece of bread. Lewis tossed it aside since it was bad, but he was not allowed anything more to eat. The Maliseet's son had a larger piece that he couldn't finish. He dropped it as he fell asleep and Lewis eagerly gobbled it up. "The little Indian awoke in the morning, and looked for his bread. It was gone. Lewis had taken it."[22] "The father…was exasperated and sentenced him to be put to death at an Indian dance to be held in the village. He went afishing…when a gale [came] up, the canoe was upset and he was drowned. By this intervention of Providence his [Lewis'] life was spared—the squaws were always kind to him and were opposed to his death and ever afterwards treated him well. He remembered the squaw with great love."[23]

The Maliseet called themselves, "Those of the river whose bed contains sparkling objects," or "People of the beautiful, good, pleasant river," referring to the 725-kilometre-long Saint John River that drains south through present-day New Brunswick to the Bay of Fundy. It was their main thoroughfare and source of food.

The neighbouring Mi'kmaq named the Maliseet tribe. In Mi'kmaq, "Maliseet" means "lazy, poor, or bad speakers" (to the Mi'kmaq, the Maliseet language sounded like faulty Mi'kmaq).[24]

The Maliseet's first European contact was in 1604, recorded by Champlain as he travelled along the banks of the Saint John River, observing these freshwater fishers and inland hunters. In the 1700s the Maliseet population numbered under one thousand.

Each spring at Aukpaque a large community of Maliseet gathered on the intervale (low bank area) for the summer months. A palisaded area protected their birchbark wigwams and long house. Women planted corn and squash, gathered and prepared food and medicine, sewed clothing, built wigwams, and cared for children. Men hunted (beaver, deer, moose, bear, and caribou), fished (salmon, bass, sturgeon, eels, and smelts), made snowshoes and canoes, and were warriors, leaders, and shamans. Children, well cared for, learned their roles from their parents, and were allowed much freedom.[25] This organized domestic life could be totally disrupted if a warrior drank alcohol. "When drunk, they stab one another, bite off each others' noses and ears and hurl their children into the fire."[26]

Another disruption of the traditional Maliseet living patterns was the pressure from the governor general to conduct raids on British territory, and from Jesuit priests to give up their traditional beliefs. (The Jesuits did such a thorough job of converting the Maliseet that they were one of the first nations to lose their aboriginal religion.)[27]

The Acadians of Sainte Anne's were probably descended from the French Roman Catholic settlers who had founded Port Royal (near present-day Digby, Nova Scotia) in 1632. France wanted a self-supporting community to anchor fur and fishing industries that would supply European markets. Around the same time, the Scots laid a rival claim to lands around the Bay of Fundy, naming it Nova Scotia (New Scotland). From then until the 1763 Treaty of Paris, international treaties referred to the area as Acadie or Nova Scotia.

For over a century, Acadian farmers cleared the Annapolis Valley and diked the salt marshes of Minas Basin and Chignecto Bay, creating fertile land. Their produce—livestock, furs, flour, oats, salt port, dried codfish, and lumber—was sold to both the British in New England and the French in Louisbourg.

At Aukpaque/Sainte Anne's, Marie Anne may have pleaded with Germain or Boishébert to return her and the children to Lunenburg. But it was not to be: this was war and they were prisoners.

Boishébert no doubt paid the warriors with presents for the scalps and prisoners. John Payzant, then six, probably mistook Boishébert to be the "Governor" when he later wrote: "ten Indians from the River Saint John…took my mother and her four children away with them to the River Saint John, where we were all ransomed by the Governor."[28]

It was probably Boishébert who told Marie Anne that she and other captives (but not her children) would go to Quebec, a nine-day trek of six hundred kilometres. Perhaps he felt remorse for his actions, which had led to her husband's death, and not wanting a French bourgeoise to become a Maliseet slave, decided to send her to Quebec. Or maybe the serious food shortage was reason enough to send all the captives off quickly.

To release her children from their new adoptive parents would have been next to impossible, however. They would have to stay in Aukpaque, be raised by the Maliseet, and taught the Roman Catholic religion by Jesuit priests. What a heartbreaking situation for Marie Anne—she might never see her children again, and they would become Roman Catholic—lost to her forever.

The next portion of the trek was by portage to the Madawaska River, which flows into Lake Temiscouata. The final portage was from the northern end of that lake to the Saint Lawrence River, where they paddled southwest to Quebec City.

Approaching Quebec by canoe, Marie Anne noticed the outline of church spires, windmills, and a hillside fort far above her, and a street winding down the hill to various buildings below. By now she was physically exhausted and concerned about her pregnancy. Sickened over Louis' death, angry over her lost liberty, and frightened, she was also relieved at the thought of being in a civilized atmosphere, and rehearsing in her mind the conversation she would have with the Roman Catholic authorities.

CHAPTER SIX

Quebec Captivity
(1756–1760)

L ikely around the end of May 1756, Marie Anne arrived with
other prisoners in the capital of New France, Quebec.[1] (*Quebecq*
is native for "the narrowing of the river.")[2] Dirty, her clothes in
tatters, she longed to rest her head on a clean, soft pillow.

Quebec, a town of eight thousand, was 146 years old when Marie
Anne arrived. The founder, Samuel de Champlain, built his trading
post near the river, recognizing the advantages of the location: an easily defended height of land on the shore of the St. Lawrence River
where the St. Charles River joins it. No enemy ship could navigate the
deep-water channel without being within range of the cannons on the
ridge. Quebec (today's Quebec City) was one of New France's three
major settlements—the others were Montreal and Trois-Rivières. A
quarter of the colony's population lived in these three towns.

Quebec housed administrators, civil servants, officers, soldiers, merchants, and craftsmen, and was a busy port from April to October, when
the river was free of ice. Supplies and settlers arrived mostly from
France, and furs or timber were exported to France or the West Indies.

In the Upper Town, the governor general, the bishop, and the intendant all lived in palatial residences surrounded by extensive formal gardens. The wealthy and the religious communities enjoyed their large
gardens, too. All imitated the genteel lifestyle of the mother country.
The Lower Town was the business centre, populated by merchants, ship
captains, shippers, artisans, and prostitutes for the sailors.

A visitor to Quebec in 1749, Swedish botanist Peter Kalm spent five
months in New France conducting scientific research. The thirty-three-
year-old's botanical and societal observations were meticulously

"A General View of Quebec, from Point Levy, Quebec, Quebec, 1761" by Richard Short.

recorded in his travel journal. He described Quebec's road from the Upper Town to the Lower Town:

> "[it is] very steep, although it is serpentine. However, people go up and down it in carriages and with wagons....Most of the merchants live in the lower city, where the houses are built very close together. The streets in it are very narrow, very rough, and almost always wet....The upper city is inhabited by people of quality, by several persons belonging to the different offices, by tradesmen, and others. In this part are the chief buildings of the town...."[3]

Kalm continues, describing the townspeople:

> [The men] are extremely civil, and take their hats off to every person indifferently whom they meet in the streets. The women in general are handsome; they are well bred and virtuous, with an innocent and becoming freedom. They dress out very fine on Sundays...[and] are very fond of adorning their heads, the hair of which is always curled and powdered and ornamented with glittering bodkins [ornamental hairpins] and aigrettes [sprays of feathers or gems].

[Ladies] are not very industrious. The young ladies, especially those of a higher rank, get up at seven and dress till nine, drinking their coffee at the same time. When they are dressed, they place themselves near a window that opens into the street, take up some needlework and sew a stitch now and then, but turn their eyes into the street most of the time.[4]

In a town where women outnumbered men, these young ladies had to look presentable, put themselves on display, and keep an eye on the eligible bachelors or wealthy widowers passing by outside.

The upper class French, described by an Englishman, were "extremely vain and have an utter contempt for the trading part of the Colony, tho' they made no scruple to engage in it, pretty deeply too, whenever a convenient opportunity served."[5]

Marie Anne arrived in Quebec at almost the same time as the new commander of France's North American military efforts: forty-seven-year-old Lieutenant-General Louis-Joseph de Montcalm, Marquis de Montcalm, seigneur de Saint-Veran, Candiac, Tournemine, Vestric, Saint-Julien, et Arpaon, Baron de Gabriac. (His pomposity was reputed to match the length of his titles.)

Montcalm was an able leader, yet he did not fit in well in New France. He longed to be home in the south of France on his estate in Candiac with his beloved wife and children, strolling among the olive groves and almond trees. But duty called. Arrogant, ambitious, and sarcastic, he was a "portly little aristocrat with a lively face and alert eyes and as passionate as befits one born in the south of France…vain, tactless, and opinionated…[and a] pessimist."[6]

Though Montcalm's father was raised a Huguenot, and descended from several generations of Huguenot nobles, he abjured in order to marry.[7] No doubt Montcalm would have been embarrassed to admit his father's former religious affiliation. Montcalm's mother, a fervent Catholic, exerted a very strong influence over him, even after he was married. It was she who convinced him to honour the king and serve his country by accepting the position in New France.

Once in the colony, several allied Indian chiefs addressed Montcalm: "We thought your head would be lost in the clouds but you are a little man, my Father. Yet when we look into your eyes we see the height of the pinetree and the fire of the eagle."[8] The description would have appealed to his vanity.

Marie Anne did not want to be in Quebec—she was there against her will—but at least she was alive. She was also no longer part of a family, which was the basic organization for social and economic purposes in the eighteenth century. Men and women remarried quickly after being widowed. Without a husband for financial stability and status, and no children to complete a family, she must have wondered how she would support herself until the baby was born and whether she would ever see her four children again.

She did have some things in her favour. Having been raised and married into the bourgeoisie in France, she would have spoken well and had a certain bearing, although her ragged clothes would have belied this. She had experience in the fabric trade and knew the business. The fact that she could sign her name indicated some education, as only ten percent of New France citizens could perform this simple task.[9]

The Maliseet delivered their captives to the government authorities, who then had to decide what to do with them. Men were often sent to the prison, and women were usually taken in by religious communities. "Some [captives] were imprisoned; others were more loosely held in seminaries, nunneries, or hospitals; still others joined private households; and at least a few were left to shift entirely for themselves."[10]

When the prisons became overcrowded, captives became servants in the homes of townspeople. In this role, they often lived a semi-free life, and if well-treated, it was hoped they would refuse to return to their previous homes when offered their freedom in the form of an exchange of prisoners by the British and French.

There is no record of where Marie Anne was lodged during her four-year stay. According to one son she was "allowed all the indulgence that could be allotted to prisoners."[11] There are a few possibilities. She may have become a servant in a private home, or lodged in one of the three religious communities of women that assumed responsibility for public charity, helping the poor, old, sick, mentally ill, prostitutes, orphans, and women prisoners. The General Hospital and the Hotel-Dieu also took in the sick, aged, mentally ill, and prostitutes.

The most likely place for Marie Anne was the Ursuline Convent. Established in Quebec in 1639 (at the request of the Jesuits) by nuns from Tours, France, the Company of Saint Ursula had been founded a century earlier in Italy and was transformed into a religious order in 1612.

The prime mission of the Ursuline Convent was to instruct the colonists' daughters and convert the native girls. The latter must have been a challenge, as in 1668 they were described as being docile and thoughtful, but quick to climb the fence and take off into the bush to join their relatives.[12] At the beginning of the eighteenth century, native

"A View of the Orphan's or Urseline [sic] Nunnery, taken from the Ramparts, Quebec, 1761" by Richard Short. Marie Anne may have stayed here from 1756 to 1760.

student enrolment declined, forcing the Ursulines to devote themselves solely to the education of the French girls. At the time that Marie Anne would have arrived, the convent housed fifty nuns, sixty boarding girls, and about 150 day students.

During this period, prejudice against girls' education meant that the nuns had to use caution. "Access to knowledge," it was believed, "would overheat the feminine spirit and result in the destruction of morals from the reading of sinful books, combined with the propensity towards such female faults as speaking too much, meddling in everything and being argumentative."[13]

The nuns had many sources of income: dowries for new nuns, room and board for girls (and some widows), and earnings from their handiwork. In 1702, the going rate for a dowry at the convent was three thousand livres.[14] Wealthy parents paid for their daughters' room and board, and there were bursaries for less affluent families. The Ursulines were well-known for their decorative work: boxes embroidered with porcupine quills; pearl arts; lacework; embroidery with silk, gold, and silver threads; painting; and gilding sculptures with gold leaf.

Girls entering the convent from wealthy families brought the required dowry and were entitled to become choir nuns. They led the services, taught students, and did administrative work. Poor girls became lay nuns who paid for their dowry in kind by looking after the choir nuns and doing the gardening, cooking, washing, and housework.

Upper class girls left the convent school to marry well. (One girl became the wife of a governor general. Later she left her family in New France for five years to be an assistant governess to the royal children in Versailles.) After finishing school, those day students without suitable spouses often returned to the convent to become nuns.

Students were taught primarily religious education, as well as reading, writing, arithmetic, history, geography, science, music, and social graces. They were probably also taught not to speak too much, not to meddle in affairs, or be argumentative.

Marie Anne may have met the superior, Marie Anne de la Nativité, born in Montreal 71 years earlier, and if she had been at the convent she would most certainly have met Sister Esther Marie Joseph de l'Enfant Jésus, a sixty-year-old nun who had been captured by Abenaki Indians in Massachusetts as a child.[15]

Born Esther Wheelwright in 1696, she was abducted in 1703 from her parents' home in Wells, Massachusetts (now in Maine), and taken to an Abenaki settlement in Massachusetts. There, French missionaries instructed her in the Roman Catholic faith. Five years later, her parents (her father was a member of the Massachusetts council) learned of her whereabouts from a captured Wells officer imprisoned in Montreal. He had spoken to the governor general, who promised to redeem him and Esther if the Massachusetts governor would return two Indian prisoners. A Jesuit priest was sent from Montreal to ransom Esther from the Abenaki, a delicate mission since the Indians were usually reluctant to give up adopted children. The Abenaki did release her. However, for unknown reasons, she was returned to Quebec, not Wells.

In Quebec, the governor general treated her with special consideration because he mistakenly believed she was a governor's daughter. He placed her in the Ursuline boarding school with his own daughter and paid for both. At fifteen, she asked to become a nun. She got her wish three years later and refused to return to her parents. Her family, however, never gave up hope that she would return.

In 1745, Sister Esther wrote to her newly widowed mother. Since she could no longer speak English, the letter had to be translated. "You know my dear Mother that the Lot which I have chosen hath

"A View of the Bishop's House with the Ruins as they appear in going down the Hill from the Upper to the Lower Town, Quebec, 1761" by Richard Short.

been that of consecrating myself wholly unto the Lord....Thus you See my lovely Mother the impossibility there is of complying with the desire you have of my return to you....I am greatly affected with the news of the death of my father, whom I loved so tenderly, and whom I shall never forget, and I shall always share with you in the trouble of so grievous a seperation."[16]

Occasionally her nephews visited and brought news of her family. In 1754, Nathaniel Wheelwright of Boston, a major involved in the exchange of prisoners, visited Sister Esther, his aunt. He wrote the following:

> I was very politely received...and Genteely entertained with Variety of wines and sweetmeats, the next morning they sent me a Genteel desart. They are conveniently Lodged, each one hath her separate appartment, with a small bed, a table, & one Chair, nothing but what is necessary, the Church is very handsomly adorned, and their Chapels, in which are very curious embroidery, all of their own work.[17]

Nathaniel gave her a miniature of her mother, framed in silver and engraved with the family arms.

In the same convent, but a prisoner of war, Marie Anne would have lived in even more modest quarters. She may have earned her keep by assisting with the bookkeeping, since she had a background in business.

We do know for certain that Marie Anne was determined to regain her children from their captivity in Acadia. Possibly through the kindness of Sister Esther, she appealed to Bishop Pontbriand,[18] the one person who had connections with Father Charles Germain and the Jesuit mission in Sainte Anne's, where as far as she knew, her children were still held captive.

Bishop Henri-Marie Dubreil de Pontbriand, born in Brittany, France, received his doctorate from the Sorbonne in Paris. In 1741, at age thirty-three, he was appointed bishop of Quebec by King Louis XV. Once in Quebec, Pontbriand wrote to Versailles, recommending that Protestants be banned from the colony: "The spiritual welfare of my diocese requires that none should be accepted....I even believe I can add that the good of the state is consistent with this view."[19] Pontbriand is described as having a warm heart and eager soul, who did not want to displease anyone, especially his superiors.

He may have sympathized with Marie Anne's plight, but his prime interest was to get her to abjure. As long as she promised to raise her children in the Catholic faith, he would agree to try to regain them through the Jesuits.

Though the Catholic persecution of Huguenots in France was the very reason she had left her native country over seventeen years earlier, at this point, she was desperate enough to acquiesce. All she had to do was put her signature on a piece of paper and make the sign of the cross. No one would know that in her heart she would always be a Huguenot.

In December she abjured at Notre-Dame de Quebec:

> The eighth day of December 1756, by virtue of the commission given by the Bishop of Quebec, our curate of Quebec, undersigned, received the abjuration of the *Religion Prétendice-Réformée* [Alleged Reformed Religion, or Huguenot religion] and the profession of the Catholic, Apostolic and Roman Religion given by Dlle [Demoiselle] Anne Noget, age 45 years, native of the village of Condé, in lower Normandy, wife (widow) of Mr. Louis Pézant; and given to her absolution of the blame incurred by the heretical profession [Huguenot religion]; and this in presence of Mr. Mathieu Dumont, of Françoise Sanson his wife, and of Félicité Migneron, wife of Jean

Abjuration of Marie Anne (Noget) Payzant, Quebec, December 8, 1756.

Spénard, who have declared not knowing how to sign [their signatures]. The aforementioned Dlle Anne Noget signed with us.
[signed] Anne Noget
[signed] Matthieu Dumont
[signed] J.F. Récher, Curate of Quebec[20]

The reference to her as "Dlle" (Demoiselle) confirms her status in the ranks of the bourgeoisie. The title "Madame" was then reserved for married women of the upper class.[21]

Perhaps Marie Anne had met these witnesses during her six months in Quebec: they were near her own age, merchants of the bourgeoisie, and probably Huguenots. (Abjuration witnesses were not required to be Roman Catholics).[22] Quebec merchants "preferred to form partnerships and other trading relationships with relatives and with people of the same religion."[23] Intendant Bigot defended the Protestant merchants against Bishop Pontbriand's prejudice on the grounds that they were harmless in religion and indispensable in trade with France.

The witness Mathieu Dumont may have been the Quebec Dumont who was an agent for a merchant from La Rochelle in France. His wife Françoise was fifty-five, a former widow.

Forty-seven-year-old witness Félicité Migneron was the third wife of sixty-two-year-old Quebec-born *cordonnier* (shoemaker) Jean Spénard.[24] He had been widowed twice.

Thirty-two-year-old Jean-Félix Récher had been the parish priest of Quebec for seven years. Norman-born (in Rouen), he was only twenty-five when he was chosen as the parish priest.[25] Perhaps having a fellow Norman perform the abjuration made it less painful for Marie Anne.

The baby she had successfully carried for nine months was born on December 26, 1756, in Quebec, no doubt attended by the parish midwife (a position elected by the parish women). This would have been a dangerous eighth birth for her, given her age of forty-five.

In some sense, this last child was a miracle. Marie Anne's other four living children were four to ten years old. Her first three had been dead for ten and twelve years. At forty-five, she was five years past the usual age of menopause at that time, and she had survived months of horrendous experiences. During her Maliseet captivity she must have taken some comfort from the fact that she was carrying a part of Louis with her—no one could take that away. No wonder she broke with the tradition of giving her daughter the first name of the godmother, and instead named her after the baby's late father.

Louise Catherine Payzant (always called "Lisette") was baptized at the Roman Catholic Cathedral, Notre-Dame de Quebec (by law all children in Quebec had to be baptized in the Catholic Church):

> The 27th December 1756 by our undersigned vicar was baptized
> Louise Catherine, born the preceding day of the legitimate mar-
> riage of the late Louis Paisant and of Anne Noget his spouse. The
> godfather was Mr. Pierre Jehanne, wholesaler of this town, and the
> godmother, Demoiselle Catherine Treffles Rotot, undersigned.
> [signed] P. Jehanne
> [signed] Catherine Treffles Rotot
> [signed] Vizien, vicar[26]

The vicar, assistant to parish priest Récher, was Philippe-Joseph Vizien. French-born, he only stayed in Quebec for five years.[27] The godparents were husband and wife, merchants, bourgeois, and definitely not Huguenots. (Godparents had to be Roman Catholic.)[28] Fifty-eight-year-old Pierre Jehanne was a merchant; Catherine Treffles Rotot was his second wife.[29]

Marie Anne apparently sent Lisette to a nursemaid, a common custom for the bourgeoisie. In 1892 a descendant remarked that Marie Anne "had never nursed any of her children and when she was delivered of Lisette...she was terribly put to it to care for her babe and some ladies at a hall...learning of it and her former life of affluence subscribed liberally at the hall and secured her a wet nurse."[30]

Marie Anne longed for the day that she would be reunited with her other children and they finally arrived in Quebec in the summer of 1757,[31] along with other captives. They had been ransomed from the Maliseet by Father Germain, who followed Bishop Pontbriand's recommendation to refuse absolution to the native adoptive parents. At one point in the negotiations, the Jesuits had been able to ransom only two of Marie Anne's children. The other Maliseet parents had temporarily refused to give up Philip and Mary.

Years later, John Payzant "vividly recalled how the beads were poured out on a blanket, when, as a child of seven years old, the Indians sold him to the priests."[32] As a teenager in Nova Scotia, John went to Windsor "and was there some time a languattor [interpreter] for the Indians as I had learnt that Languages when prisoner among them, and I spent some time in Cornwallis in the Same maner."[33] The Maliseet language that he learned at Aukpaque is part of the Eastern Algonquian language, as is Mi'kmaq in Nova Scotia. Both nations understand each other.

The children spent almost a year living with the Maliseet, but there are no records as to whether they were well-treated and loved, or used as slaves. They might have even witnessed enemy Mohawk or British captives being tortured. One wonders how far the Jesuits got in their efforts to convert them, and just how much their early experiences later affected their lives and relationships. A strong clue is provided in John's autobiography, written at the age of sixty-one, in which he powerfully describes his emotional instability as a young adult.

When the children arrived in Quebec in 1757, Marie Anne may have had to pay ransom. It's not known whether she was allowed to spend time with them, or whether they were dispersed to various religious communities. Mary, aged nine, may have been allowed to enter the Ursuline convent as a boarder and live under the same roof as her mother. Possibly Marie Anne had to pay for her room and board.

The boys were probably lodged in the Quebec seminary and sent to the Jesuit college. The college originated in 1635 when the Jesuits opened an infant school for the colonists' sons. Education was free,

"A View of the Jesuits College and Church, Quebec, 1761" by Richard Short. John Payzant attended here from 1756 to 1760.

but room and board cost ten livres per month. The subjects taught were catechism, reading, writing, arithmetic, history, French grammar, and geography. The college was the only school in Quebec to offer complete primary and secondary education. It closed from 1759 to 1761 following the fighting between the British and French. Even though British soldiers took over the building, the primary school continued to operate until 1776.

Father Germain, the European-educated missionary at Sainte Anne's in Acadia, wrote of the Jesuit College: "everything…is done as in our colleges in Europe, and perhaps with greater attention to rules and greater rigour and with better results than in many of our colleges in France."[34]

In 1757 John (aged seven) attended the Jesuit College, but I don't know whether Philip or Louis (ten and six) did as well. The college student list disappeared after the British conquest in 1759.[35] It is known, however, that Louis was taught by a priest in 1759.[36]

John wrote of his time in Quebec: "I was sent to the Jesuits to be instructed in the Learning of that Academy and during my stay there I made great proficiency in the Arts that were taught in that School, and as they were fond to proselyte they took the more pains with me."[37] He recalled learning Latin and French.

Food was in short supply for everyone throughout New France during most of Marie Anne's time in Quebec. Bread, the staple of their diet, was rationed due to poor harvests and irregular wartime flour shipments from France. Sometimes oats and peas were mixed with flour to extend it. In front of the cathedral, "A few minutes after eight Father Récher and Madame Lefebvre arrived with baskets of bread, which they distributed according to Bigot's instructions. The mothers hid the food in the large pockets of their capes. The children wanted more, but Madame Lefebvre had no more to give."[38]

In December 1757, since beef and pork had become scarce in the towns, the government distributed horsemeat. The townspeople disliked it, however, and some militant Montreal women marched to the governor's residence, threw the horsemeat at his door, and said they'd rather die than eat it because the horse was a friend to man.

In Quebec, soldiers were issued a rotation of horsemeat for three days, beef for three, and codfish for two. Montcalm set an example by having horsemeat served at his own table. He wrote of various options: "Small horse meat patties, Spanish style; horse meat stew; scalloped horse meat; horse meat steak on the spit with a good pepper and vinegar sauce; horses' feet baked in bread crumbs; hashed horse tongue with onions; horse meat ragout; smoked horse tongue, better than that of moose; horse meat pie, like hare pie. This animal is much better than moose, caribou and beaver."[39] I wonder which ways Marie Anne and the nuns preferred.

As hostilities grew between the French and British, Quebec's population swelled with starving Acadians, habitants forced off their farms, large numbers of British military prisoners, shiploads of French soldiers (some of whom brought illness; five hundred ending up in the General Hospital), and Indians of various nations who helped the French raid British forts.

While the people went hungry, the intendant threw lavish all-night balls during *Carnaval* (Shrove Tuesday), when large sums were gambled away.

Quebec curate Jean-Félix Récher recorded spine-chilling Indian atrocities in his journal, which sound so gruesome that one wonders if they're accurate. In June 1757 "barbarous savages cut two English prisoners in pieces...and put them in their cooking pot."[40] In July, "Ten English were massacred by the savages...in a game; 4 others were disembowelled and their blood drunk by the savages."[41] At the end of August, "3 or 400 English...[were] ransomed from the

Savages by the French."[42] (That would have been a major drain on the coffers.) The next spring "They carried back 40 scalps...and brought back 3 prisoners."[43] The French regarded their native allies as barbarians, cruel beyond belief, and were appalled by the cannibalism of certain nations.[44]

In June 1759 Lewis Payzant witnessed the arrival of British ships, initially with excitement. "He well recollected the sight of the British Fleet entering the Harbour. Three or four men of war ships lay off in sight two or three days before all the fleet got up [a formidable fleet of more than 200 ships]. At the commencement of the siege [in July] he was being taught in the Priest's Office...a boom shell came crashing through the roof of the house which cut off the fuse—it fell into the cellar and did not explode."[45]

The siege had begun. On the evening of July 12, the British bombarded Quebec from their batteries just over one kilometre away on the other side of the river. All night, townspeople trundled carts of bedding and food to the ramparts. The next morning they fled to the countryside. Even the Ursuline convent was hit. In mid-July everyone in the convent (except for ten nuns, a chaplain, and two priests who remained on guard) took refuge at the General Hospital,[46] outside of the town and well out of cannon range.

The tall and energetic Mother Superior of the hospital was an aunt of Boishébert, a sister of his mother. She and her staff, caring for hundreds of desperate people, "lodged them in the sheds. Her employees emptied the barns of cattle and turned them into dormitories for mothers and their young children. They themselves doubled up so that elderly couples could use their quarters. More people were housed in the attics...[they] even had the laundry rooms converted into living accommodations, making it difficult for the nuns to wash the much-needed linens. Early in the morning, [the Mother Superior] had gone out to meet more than thirty Ursuline nuns who had had to abandon their convent. She gave them the rooms of her sisters, reserving her own sitting-room for the mother abbess of the Ursulines."[47]

Throughout July and August of 1759, the British continued to fire cannons on Quebec, trying to force the French out into battle. A contemporary diarist noted an unusually large number of July thunderstorms, which would have added to the cacophony. The cathedral was destroyed and the centre of town burned. In August a great fire engulfed the Lower Town, destroying 180 homes. Luckily most of the inhabitants had already fled to the countryside.

Marie Anne's three sons were apparently not evacuated, because ten-year-old John witnessed the Battle of the Plains of Abraham on

Rue du Petit-Champlain, Lower Town, Quebec, 2002.

September 13, 1759: "Old men, women, children, and all men not bearing arms lined the streets and the ramparts of Quebec watching the soldiers from Beauport marching through their town, with flags flying and drums beating. The regulars were all dressed in their white uniforms, the colonial troops in the long greyish-white coats, blue breeches, and stockings, and the militia in their everyday clothes...The Indians...[were] covered in war-paint, a single feather on their heads, and their tomahawks and knives among the scalps hanging from their waists."[48]

A light rain was falling, so Lewis might have slipped a few times as he scrambled up the grassy slopes to the stone walls surrounding the city. Looking southwest over the plains, he would have seen the backs of the French forces advancing in formation less than a kilometre away toward the British thin red line, each side numbering about four thousand, five hundred. Flanking them on the hills were French Canadian soldiers and Indian allies from several nations. Lewis Payzant's interviewer recorded this account:

> On the morning of that day...several boys had climbed upon that part of the wall of the city which overlooked the Plains of Abraham....They were discovered by the military guard, who immediately ordered them down. One of them [John Payzant] refused to obey, and the attention of the guard being immediately directed to matters of more importance, the refractory youth was suffered to remain in quiet possession of his post. The object at which he was gazing with so much eagerness was a battle. Two hostile armies were engaged in fierce and dreadful encounter upon the Plains of Abraham. It was the day of the taking of Quebec by General Wolfe.[49]

The battle was short—only about fifteen minutes. John may have been alone among his friends in secretly wishing for a British victory, so he could return to Nova Scotia. Soon the French soldiers broke ranks and started running north towards the bridge to Beauport or back through the city gates.

Montcalm rode his black horse toward the St. Louis gate but was shot. Some of his men propped him up on his horse (so as not to raise alarm) and led him to a doctor's house, just off rue de St. Louis. He died at five o'clock the next morning and was buried in a bomb crater inside the Ursuline chapel.

Five days after the battle, Quebec formally surrendered. John would have noticed the British redcoats now guarding the city gates. He was probably wondering what was to become of him and his brothers—whether or not they would be reunited with their mother and sisters (likely still at the General Hospital), and, very importantly, whether they would get more food.

Marie Anne and the children weren't able to leave Quebec for another eight months or so. They would suffer through food shortages in the now-destroyed town, and put up with the chaos of the change of command to Brigadier-General James Murray. It was September. The river would soon freeze. No supply ships would arrive until spring. Yet somehow they survived.

By the end of September, the Ursulines were able to return to the convent from their refuge at the General Hospital. However, the convent was unfit for use in winter and they were reduced to abject poverty. But Murray needed the nuns to care for his wounded soldiers (at the king's expense), so he got funding for repairs to the building.

By the beginning of October, the wounded were moved in and tended by the nuns. The Ursulines adapted to their new task as hospital nuns and even knitted long woollen stockings for the bare legs of the Scottish soldiers.[50] However, more than their legs were bare: "After an ice-storm in January [1760], the kilted Frasers reached their guard posts in Lower Town by sliding down Mountain Street on bare behinds. Such sights upset the nuns, who began knitting long woollen drawers for the Highlanders."[51] The recuperated soldiers left in June 1760.

The convent's restored chapel was the only building suitable for use as a parish church. Protestant services for the British soldiers were held alternately with Roman Catholic services. On November 8, 1759, parish priest Récher sought refuge at the convent—he had been robbed and wounded by a fanatical British soldier the previous night on his way home to the seminary. He stayed for five years, holding services in the chapel, before moving back to the seminary.[52]

At long last, the spring of 1760 arrived, breaking up the ice and allowing ships to dock. Marie Anne and her five children were finally able to sail away from Quebec. They apparently travelled with members of the Perrotte[53] family, who may have been Huguenot prisoners of war. Perhaps they were related to the merchant Perrotte in Caen who had rented Louis' shop after he fled in 1739. If so, it must have been a comfort for Marie Anne to be with someone who had known her late husband.

CHAPTER SEVEN

Falmouth, Another Beginning
(1761–1796)

Seven long years had passed since Marie Anne first stepped onto the dock at Halifax. On that day in 1753 she and Louis had arrived from Jersey with four children, full of hope for a prosperous life in a new land. Now, arriving from war-torn Quebec, she was bedraggled and weary with five children in tow. She heaved a sigh of relief to be back in Nova Scotia with no more restrictions on her life.

She apparently stayed in Halifax over the winter of 1760, possibly with the Perrotte[1] family, with whom she could speak French and discuss their ordeal in Quebec. Survival over the winter must have been difficult—perhaps the government provided for her.

Louis' Lunenburg properties and islands were hers now, but in light of the tragedy on Payzant's Island, she refused to return. In the spring of 1761, she decided to take a free grant of land in Falmouth, a new township in the Pisiquid area on the Minas Basin. The Board of Trade in London wanted that area of rich farmland and diked marshes, now vacated by Acadians, to be populated by Protestant New Englanders.

"Full liberty of conscience" was assured "to persons of all persuasions, Papists excepted."[2] In May 1760, two sloops of fifty-eight settlers arrived from Rhode Island in the first wave of New England "Planters" (an old English term for those who "planted" colonies).

Marie Anne and the children likely took the overland route from Halifax to Falmouth in 1761, accompanied by armed soldiers for protection. Acadians (those who had escaped the expulsion) and their allies, the Mi'kmaq, still frequently raided the British settlements in that area, incited by their French priests.

This route, originally an Acadian cattle-driving path from Halifax, had been widened to eighteen feet in 1749 at the request of Governor Cornwallis, and was improved by Governor Lawrence in 1760. The road was "merely a strip from which the trees had been cut down, with a footpath making its way between the stumps, and at the most something in the way of log footbridges over streams and possibly some laying of poles across the worst unavoidable swamps."[3]

Tradition states that while riding horseback to Falmouth, Marie Anne noticed a rattlesnake, killed it, and took the rattles with her.[4]

Once at Falmouth East (renamed Windsor in 1764) on the east side of the Pisiquid River (renamed the Avon River in 1764), she may have recognized Fort Edward on the hill. Seeing the British redcoats on duty at the fort five years earlier had prompted the Maliseet to threaten her if she didn't keep quiet. To reach Falmouth West (renamed Falmouth in 1764), they would have forded the Pisiquid River at low tide.

Until Marie Anne's land grants were finalized, the family likely stayed at Falmouth West's newly built Fort Lawrence (located at the "upland between both marshes" and in sight of Fort Edward).[5] On July 21, 1761, a formal grant gave her a five hundred-acre farm lot (No. 47, First Division), a six-acre town lot (No. 1B in Second Division), a ten-acre dike lot (No. 3E in the Great Falmouth Marsh), and one hundred acres in condemned lots.[6] Under the terms of the grant, the properties had to be improved.

At last she had a place of her own in a new community of fellow Protestants, and a base from which her children could thrive and put their four years of captivity and hard times behind them. But first they had to learn how to farm and how to speak and write English. The older children—Philip, thirteen; Mary, twelve; John, ten; and Lewis, nine—wouldn't have remembered English from the time they lived in Jersey and Lunenburg. Lisette, three, had never learned it.

In August 1761, she was given formal title to Louis' Lunenburg islands. It read: "...unto Mary Paysant her Heirs and Assigns a Tract of Land Situate lying and being an Island in Mahone Bay called Payzants Island containing one hundred Acres or thereabouts, One other Island lying to the South East of the Same containing about forty Acres, Also a thirty Acre lot Number Eight in Oakland in the Said Bay containing in the whole by Estimation One hundred and Seventy Acres being in the Township of Lunenburg with all and all manner of Mines unopened, etc. etc. etc."[7] (Louis' original thirty-acre lot was number four, not eight. This may have been a clerical error.)

On August 18, Jonathan Belcher, "President of His Majesty's Council & Commander in Chief, etc. etc. etc.," issued Marie Anne a

Fort Edward blockhouse, Windsor, Nova Scotia, 1997.

licence to sell the Lunenburg properties. "Whereas Mary Peaysant [sic] hath by humble Petition applied to me for Licence to dispose of two Island[s] and a Thirty Acre Lot granted to her in the Township of Lunenburg thereby to raise a Sum of Money to enable her to improve and Stock certain Lands granted to her in the Township of Falmouth, and to assist in maintaining a numerous family...."[8]

But Marie Anne did not immediately sell the two islands, or the Lunenburg town lot with its house, or the quarter-acre garden plot. Her eldest son Philip, almost fifteen, might have expressed interest in them.

Marie Anne's Falmouth West town lot may have contained an Acadian log house.[9] While the Acadian buildings in Grand Pré were burned after the 1755 expulsion, the ones in Pisiquid were left untouched. As a widow with children, she might have been given an already constructed house. She no doubt lived there for a few years until another could be built on her farm lot.[10]

In 1762 Falmouth West, Marie Anne and her children were one of eighty families comprising 350 residents. She was then fifty-one and her eldest son fifteen. They wouldn't have been able to operate a farm to support themselves and the other four children. As a property owner, however, she made an attractive widow for an eligible man.

The man who came along was Irishman Malachi Caigin. His given name appears also as Meloky and Malacky. However, his surname has many more variations: Caigen, Caigan, Caggin, Cagan, Caggan, Cagen, Caggen, Cagghorn, Clagghorn, Cazen, Kagen, Keagan, and Kegon. Eighteenth-century scribes certainly didn't concern themselves with consistent spelling!

Caigin had moved initially to New England, then to Cornwallis in about 1760 with the Connecticut Planters.[11] Most of the surviving records that mention him show he was repeatedly on the wrong side of the law. In June 1761 in Cornwallis, he did "profanely Curse, Swear and threaten" two men. He pursued them with a crowbar saying to one "Damn You, I'll Splitt you Down."[12] On the Lord's Day in September, along with three others, he "Did ride Extravagantly, hallow & Scream greatly to the Disturbance of the People & being asked…why they so behaved on the Sabbath, answered for their Pleasure."[13]

One year later in Falmouth West, "Malachi Kagen was married with the widow Mary Payzant September ye 15th Anno Domi 1762."[14] The Church of England, the official church of the time, occasionally sent out ministers to the new settlements. Reverend Thomas Wood, assistant minister in Halifax, visited Falmouth West twice in 1762. Probably on his second visit he married Marie Anne and Malachi.

In 1763 Caigin opened a tavern in Falmouth West, where in March he and six others got into a brawl at "the House of Mr. Malachy Cagan Inholder at Falmouth."[15] Three patrons argued violently and Caigin, "imployed in the affairs of the House did not so Minutely take notice of the Matter,"[16] asked the ringleader to leave the premises. When outside, the fellow struck and kicked Caigin leaving "both his Hand and Shin [to] bleed considerably."

It must have been a marriage of convenience—Marie Anne was no doubt desperate. Caigin would have been very pleased, since her property was now listed under his name. The first decade in Falmouth couldn't have been very easy for Marie Anne. Now a newly wed wife of a rowdy tavern owner and mother of five children who were adjusting to life in a new environment, she had her hands full. However, Caigin may have been a major help in building the farmhouse, cutting hay for the cattle, and planting corn, flax, and root vegetables in fields that had already been cultivated by the Acadians.

In November 1763, Philip Payzant (then seventeen) was living in Lunenburg. Perhaps he had clashed with his new stepfather and moved out to live in the house on the Lunenburg town lot, which was still registered to "Luis Pesant."

Payzant genealogist Marion M. Payzant states that a French-speaking Swiss schoolteacher—John James Juhan—may have lived with the Caigins at that time, no doubt pleased to speak his native language as well as English. (Years later, he instructed music, dance, and fencing, manufactured musical instruments, and was a concert performer.) Marie Anne's older daughter, Mary, caught his eye and they were married, probably in 1764. Their twins, a girl and a boy, were born the next year in Halifax, where the couple had moved in 1765 when Mary was seventeen.

There were few schools in those years. Wealthy children were sent to Halifax, and some local children were taught by a grantee in his own home. In 1767 another teacher (the first schoolmaster sponsored by the London-based Society for the Propagation of the Gospel), reported that he had fifty students in the summer and thirty in the winter. Lewis and Lisette (then fifteen and ten) may have been among them.

John Payzant moved out in 1765, as he later wrote of being educated in Halifax by his brother-in-law (John James Juhan). John was having a difficult time trying to figure out what to do for a living. Young men at that time often apprenticed in various trades, such as tanning, brick-making, carpentry, and mill works, to name a few. He returned to Falmouth in 1769 at the age of twenty to learn husbandry, the breaking and teaching of young horses. Then he learned the tanning trade from William Alline.[17]

Troubling, too, for John, was the mental turmoil of worshiping as an English-speaking Protestant after four years' instruction as a Roman Catholic under the Quebec Jesuits. "My mind was not easy, for my futer [future] state, and imorality was my Greatest concern."[18] While he sat with a friend in a "pubblick House" someone came in talking about a man in nearby Cornwallis who had died just as he got up from his seat. "After that I dare not rise from my chair for some time tho' my friend pressed me hard to Return home. I told him I would Soon go. I often looked on the floor and though[t] if I should Rise, and fall done [down] Dead that my soul Would fall thro[u]gh the floor and go done [down] to Hell. After some time I rose up and Went home."[19]

Two shocking events for young John—seeing his father's murder and being captured by Maliseet—were likely the main reasons for his psychological frailty as a young adult. In those pioneer times, the psychological effects of traumatic events were probably not identified, or treated. Exposure to itinerant preachers left him still unsettled.

John had known Henry Alline since 1761 when they were twelve and thirteen years old. The Allines had moved from Rhode Island with the Planters in 1760 to a farm lot adjacent to Marie Anne's in Falmouth West. Henry's schooling and religious instruction ended with the move. He, too, was searching for meaning and became increasingly concerned about Mi'kmaq attacks and going to hell if he were killed. "Many came out among us," Alline wrote in his journal, circa 1780, "with their faces painted, and declared that the English should not settle this country."[20] Knowing that Indians had murdered Louis Payzant likely heightened his anxiety.

At fourteen, Henry became quite ill, and was told he would not recover. In fact he did recuperate, but the fear of death only added to his distress. As much as he enjoyed dancing at "frolicks" to Acadian fiddlers and drinking wine with his friends, he was troubled: "when I returned from my carnal mirth I felt as guilty as ever, and could sometimes not close my eyes for some hours after I had got home to my bed."[21]

In 1774 John married his friend's sister, Mary Alline, hoping that it would cure his torment, but he became even more uneasy. Henry told John that "the Lord had appeared for him in a most wonderful maner, and he believed that the Lord would appear for me."[22] The Lord did appear for John: "The joys and tranceport of my Soul, to think that I had been laboring So long for Something, and I did not know what....There came Such a thought in my mind, go, and tell what great thing the Lord hath done for you."[23]

For John, this epiphany provided the basis for the emotional security he had been seeking after the trauma of his youth and the difficult adaptation to a new life among New Englanders whose language and culture were foreign.

After Henry Alline's own epiphany (one week before John Payzant's in the spring of 1775) he believed "that the essence of Christianity was spiritual rebirth through a personal religious experience."[24] He eventually became the leader of the New Light religious movement of Nova Scotia's Great Awakening (John joined that movement too, as an itinerant minister). Begun in the 1740s in New England, the New Light church emphasized personal conversion, or the receiving of the New Light as the only way to salvation.

A charismatic, full-time itinerant minister, Alline preached with drama and passion throughout Nova Scotia. He suffered from tuberculosis, however, and drove himself to the very end of his endurance. While very ill, and on an extensive missionary tour in New Hampshire, he died at thirty-five. John lost his good friend and brother-in-law.

In August 1766, John's stepfather, Malachi Caigin, was in Halifax, probably as a drover of sheep from Falmouth to the market in Halifax. (His days as a tavern owner were no doubt over.) Caigin signed a promissory note for just over £5 to John Burbidge,[25] an Englishman who represented Cornwallis in the provincial House of Assembly. Burbidge was a popular man known for his benevolence. (Promissory notes were widely circulated in Nova Scotia due to a lack of currency at that time.) Four years later Caigin repaid £3. His estate paid the balance twelve years later. It's curious that he had been desperate enough to borrow.

By 1768 Philip Payzant, then twenty-two, was farming in Chester Township, west of Lunenburg, on the three-hundred-acre lot he had been granted at seventeen (F9 in Third Division, near present-day New Canada). He had qualified for the land by being an original grantee's son.

That same year, Philip gave a good friend a four-acre lot, number six on Oak Island.[26] This is the same Oak Island in Mahone Bay, where supposedly in the 1600s the Scottish pirate Captain Kidd buried a vast treasure in such an ingenious way that today, after many men's lives have been lost and much money has been spent, it still lies in its "Money Pit" unclaimed.

The Falmouth 1770 census lists five people in the Caigin household: one man (Caigin), two boys (likely John and Lewis, twenty and nineteen), one woman (Marie Anne, fifty-nine), and one girl (likely Lisette, thirteen).[27] Their "Stock and Substance" included four "Oxen & Bulls," three cows, five "Young neat cattle," and two pigs. Their "Produce of the last Year" showed only four bushels of "Pease." Compared with neighbours who were producing substantial crops of wheat, peas, barley, and oats, this was a poor harvest. Either Caigin was a failure as a farmer or their efforts were concentrated on livestock.

It is also possible that he and Marie Anne had separated and the four bushels of peas were all that she could muster. We know for certain that the marriage did not last, though a formal divorce was virtually impossible to obtain in Nova Scotia at that time. Perhaps Caigin moved out in 1770—the date the ownership of the dike lot granted to Marie Anne in 1761 changed over from Caigin to John Payzant.

Far away from his mother's domestic problems, twenty-five-year-old Philip Payzant was farming near Lunenburg. Legend states that one day while loading hay, he met one of the Maliseet who had killed his father.[28] A flood of emotions no doubt surged through him as he remembered the attack—he had been nine, standing on the table waving his fists in defence of his mother and siblings. Now on his farm, he gave chase with the pitchfork and attacked the Maliseet. Later, fearing a reprisal, he made preparations to leave Nova Scotia.

In 1772 the Reformed Congregation Church paid him £2 for the town lot originally granted to his father in 1753.[29] He also sold his own three hundred-acre lot, hopped a ship in the Lunenburg harbour, and sailed for Boston.

Two years later, in April 1774, Philip married Martha Hood in Boston. In 1775 he joined the American Revolutionary Army, and served in the Revolutionary War until 1777.[30] His trail ends there. The army may have been an outlet for his pent-up rage over his childhood trauma. I wonder if Marie Anne ever saw him again.

In the mid-1770s Marie Anne may have had some farm equipment repaired or oxen shod by the local blacksmith. He was thirty-year-old Francis Layton, who arrived in Falmouth with his wife and infant son as part of a wave of Yorkshire immigrants (and was another of my ancestors). He lived near present-day Bog Road, probably on rented premises, since Falmouth's lots had been fully granted by then.[31]

The year 1774 was probably a time of mixed emotions for Marie Anne. She was separated from Caigin, Philip was in Boston, and Mary was married and living in Charleston, South Carolina. Philip and John were married that year—Philip in Boston and John in Falmouth.

In Falmouth, Lisette married twenty-one-year-old George Jess. His father, Falmouth grantee Joseph Jess, was a Planter who came from New England in 1760. Originally, he had been a linen weaver in Belfast, Ireland. At nineteen, George purchased Falmouth farm lot number sixteen from his father. He remained there after his marriage to eighteen-year-old Lisette, but before 1786, they moved to Scots Bay in Cornwallis Township, where he bought land in 1792. They had seven children from 1775 to 1786. One of her granddaughters was named Mary Ann, likely after Lisette's mother.

Only Lewis remained at home with Marie Anne, but he, too, married, sometime around 1775.[32] It's probable that his wife, Grace Davison (daughter of neighbour John Davison, a Connecticut Planter), moved into Marie Anne's homestead and farmed with Lewis. Seven children were born to the couple between 1776 and 1793. Despite the busy household, Marie Anne no doubt took delight in her namesake, another Mary Ann, Lewis' first daughter, born in 1783.

Years later, as Lewis lay on his deathbed "with great emotion and with tears in his eyes" he recalled his story to his eldest son. "God has been wonderful kind to me. He has crafted me over that tremendous sea safely from my own country to America. I must make my peace with God and be happy in eternity. He has passed me through seen and unseen dangers and He will land me where the waters cease from troubling."[33]

When the American Revolution broke out in 1776, Nova Scotia had a well-established government with a popularly elected assembly, close commercial and kinship ties with New England, and a population of twenty thousand. Two-thirds of the inhabitants had either been born in New England or were first generation Nova Scotians, yet Nova Scotia sided with Britain. There were a number of reasons for this. Halifax merchants, who largely ran the assembly, were in competition with New England merchants, so the British connection was in their best interest. The settlers were also too preoccupied with survival to concern themselves with war, and their New Light evangelist Henry Alline preached against war of any kind. Nevertheless, they were all in constant fear of American raids: "There was great anxiety throughout the Minas Townships [Cornwallis, Horton and Falmouth] caused by raids by American privateers and the threat of invasions by American forces."[34]

In mid-October 1776, in the midst of this confusion, Malachi Caigin was murdered. "In a controversy with a neighbour when both were angry, he [Peter Manning], being a most powerful man, physically, struck him with a blow with a stick, and he died from the effects of it."[35]

A dispute over sheep is often cited as the incident that led to the murder. At the time, Caigin was a drover of sheep to the Halifax market—perhaps Manning was upset that Caigin kept one or two sheep for himself. Eight months later several Falmouth residents were "appointed to inspect all droves or flocks of sheep before crossing the Avon River [fording the mud flats at low tide could be dangerous— some farmers lost cattle and teams of oxen in the quicksand]. The rate of 1 penny per head was to be paid to the Falmouth inspector. Drovers were required to carry certificates with details of ear marks and numbers of the sheep sold to the drover."[36]

Peter Manning, father of six, and, like Caigin, an Irishman, probably moved from Philadelphia in the early 1770s, encouraged by his cousin Walter Manning, a Falmouth grantee of 1763. Two of Peter's Irish-born sons (James and Edward) became well-known and highly respected Baptist ministers. They had been impressionable nine- and thirteen-year-olds when their father was tried, found guilty, and hanged within weeks of the murder. The conversion of James Manning in the New Light church was due to the influence of John Payzant, none other than the stepson of the man his father had

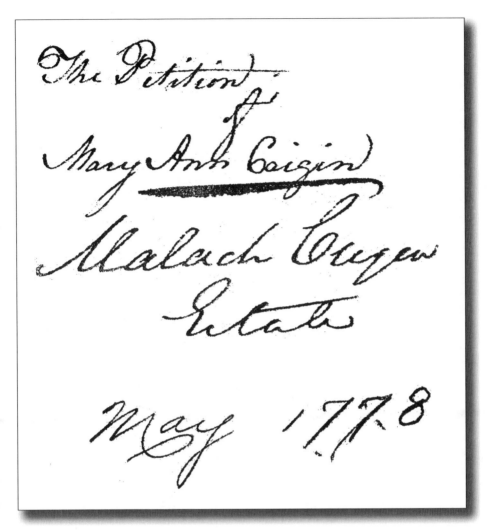

Petition of Mary Ann Caigin, Falmouth, Nova Scotia, May 1778.

killed.[37] Reverend Edward Manning was involved in the establishment of Acadia University in the 1830s.[38]

In May 1778, nineteen months after the murder, Marie Anne filed a petition to receive any money accruing from debts due Caigin's estate. The petition states that "oppressed with Age and Sickness, And for Eighteen months Successively Under the Doctors Care [she] Is now reduced to Very great Straits."[39] Seven months later she received £4.

That statement may merely have been an exaggerated bid to reclaim any monies owing to her. She probably wasn't really that ill, but she may have lost many of her land holdings and could have been financially strapped.

In 1793 her son John Payzant moved to Liverpool, Nova Scotia, where he eventually became the minister of the Old Zion Church. In his ministry work, John discovered that the Greek and Latin he learned from the Jesuits "were of Great use to me."[40] To supplement his income there, he took up the tanning business taught to him in Falmouth by William Alline, later his father-in-law. He also made shoes—a recurring object of significance in the family. (Thirty-eight pairs of shoes were brought over from Jersey by his father, and the silver wedding shoes had been carefully kept by his mother.) In Falmouth, a frail eighty-two-year-old Marie Anne would have missed him.

After a long and adventurous life, Marie Anne died in Falmouth in 1796[41] and was laid to rest in the family burial ground. Called "Mount Piziquid," it was on a high corner of her original land grant, and commanded a view of the Avon River (formerly the Pisiquid River). Her property went to her second oldest son John. Lewis was farming the property and six years later received the deed from his brother.

To live until eighty-five was rare in those days. At the time of her death, Marie Anne had been living on the Falmouth farm with her son Lewis (a farmer and local minister), his wife Grace, and their seven children.[42] Philip and Martha were somewhere in the United States. Reverend John and Mary lived in Liverpool with their nine children. Mary, wife of John James Juhan, and the mother of twins, was possibly living in Philadelphia or Saint Dominique (now Haiti). Lisette and George Jess, who were farming in nearby Scots Bay, had seven children. This expanding family lost their matriarch, but the story of Louis and Marie Anne Payzant lives on today, having been passed down through the generations.

Epilogue

To create a fuller picture of Marie Anne and Louis Payzant's lives, I needed to visit the locations that were relevant in their lives. Since my obsession with Marie Anne's life began, I've travelled to France and Jersey (British Channel Islands), as well Canadian locations: Quebec City, and in Nova Scotia, Halifax, Lunenburg, and Falmouth. I captured a sense of the geography of each place plus tidbits of information from local people. Various archives yielded wonderful information, shedding light on the lives of my ancestors.

CAEN, NORMANDY, FRANCE

Caen, with a population of 189,000, and a university founded by England's King Henry VI in the fifteenth century, is the capital of the department of Calvados, and the cultural capital of the Basse-Normandie region (Lower Normandy). Connected to the English Channel by a twelve-kilometre-long canal, it is the largest port in that half of Normandy.

Caen was at the centre of the Battle of Normandy, which lasted for over two months in 1944. After the devastating bombing raid on June 6, fire raged for eleven days, burning out the central area. Canadian troops entered Caen from the west a month later, but the Germans, who had occupied the city for four years, continued to shell it well into August. Louis Payzant would have wept to see his hometown reduced to piles of rubble.

Louis may have lived in a two-story half-timbered house, with dormer windows (from *dormir*, which means "to sleep") poking out of the steep-roofed attic facing the street. The second floor probably jutted out over the main floor. There are two theories for this over-hang design: home owners were able to get more floor space from a given foundation size; and each overhang protected the lower windows from the sun, rain, or the contents of a chamber pot dumped into the street.

On eighteenth-century Caen streets, houses sat shoulder to shoulder, each one having a main front door and a wider door for horse and carriage that led to a courtyard. Metal or wooden signs, swinging and squeaking in the breeze, hung over the road advertising the shops. Windows would have had multiple diamond- or square-shaped small panes. There was no sidewalk, but the narrow streets were paved with cobblestones that drained toward the centre.

Remarkably, two sixteenth-century houses in Caen on rue Saint Pierre survived the bombings in 1944. Built for rich merchants, the wonderful carvings on the front combine Gothic design elements (in their profusion of carved decorations and numerous statues of the saints), and Renaissance elements (the carved balustrades and medallions). Some of the carvings are religious, some are graceful scrolls around a fleur-de-lis, and one grouping shows three smiling dancers with another clapping time. It's a delightful legacy that has charmed passing pedestrians for five centuries. Louis was no doubt very familiar with these two houses on the same street as his.

The *ancienne halle* (old market hall) next door, one of the first sites of the Protestant movement, was destroyed in 1944. Now rebuilt, it's a multi-storied building with shops on the main level, adding to the atmosphere of this modern pedestrian shopping area.

In Louis' parish of Saint Pierre in Caen the thirteenth-century Saint Pierre church is dominated by a tall, spire-topped tower (rebuilt after 1944), its character derived from the riot of Renaissance ornamental stonework rising from the flying buttresses on the sides and back. Many of the ornate pinnacles and gargoyles were replaced. Today, a parking lot and an area for the Sunday market surround the back where centuries earlier women washed their laundry in the Odon River.

Across from Saint Pierre and up the hill, pock-marked stone walls (damaged in 1944) surround William the Conqueror's restored chateau, built from local stone. Thanks to William's influence, Caen stonecutters were kept busy providing the building blocks for the Tower of London, Westminster Abbey, and Canterbury Cathedral—a touch of home for the king while in England. On the grounds of the Caen chateau is the Musée de Normandie (Normandy Museum) where the Intendant De Vastan once resided.

Antoine and Suzanne Paisant lived on Notre-Dame-de-Froiderue

Saint-Pierre church, thirteenth century, Caen, France, with circular wall of eleventh-century chateau on right, 2001.

(Our Lady of Cold Street), so named due to cool air currents and the church at the corner of rue Saint Pierre, called Notre-Dame. The street first appeared in twelfth-century charters. During the fifteenth century it was known for its printing industry, handy for students since the university was nearby. Today, tucked away through narrow passageways on the street renamed rue Froide, are the courtyards and gardens of fifteenth- and sixteenth-century manor houses built for wealthy bourgeois. A wall plaque on rue Froide asks tourists to take only a discreet glance at these private courtyards.

Centuries ago the houses featured big arcades that framed shuttered stalls opening directly onto the street. Missed by the 1944 bombs, today the shops lining the cobblestoned and curved rue Froide display their wares under multi-coloured awnings. A bookstore with ancient tomes in its window reminds me of the heritage of the street. I wonder if some of those books might have been part of the eighty that Louis had left behind ("69 old volumes of which four were in-quarto, others in-octavo, in-sexto and in-douze, with eleven other calf-skin-covered volumes of little value"[1]).

At the Calvados Archives in Caen, I located the Paisant file and carefully separated the papers that I wanted to photocopy from others which were indecipherable, mostly due to worm holes still containing the dust left behind by those ancient burrowers.

In my haste to photocopy, I didn't savour the fact that I was actually holding the very letters that my ancestor had written with his quill pen 262 years earlier. Those letters, plus the request to De Vastan about Suzanne's release, had been used in the legal case against Louis. I was puzzled as to why the letters, all dated September 19, 1739 from Jersey, and addressed to four different cities in France, could be together again. Then it dawned on me that the government authorities who compiled the dossier on Louis as evidence for his trial *in absentia* would have traced down his colleagues and demanded any evidence as to his whereabouts and his financial situation. Or, the letters might have been intercepted in some way. I can just imagine the people who had handled those papers—from an anxious Louis to the pompous intendant and the pious convent superior to the gloating wigged lawyers.

CONDÉ-SUR-NOIREAU, NORMANDY, FRANCE

Payzant genealogist Marion Payzant stated in her 1970 book that Marie Anne was likely born in Caen in 1702.[2] However, from a 1756 document in Quebec, I found she was baptized in Condé-sur-Noireau in 1711. I know nothing about her family, because the relevant church records were destroyed in World War Two.

Condé-sur-Noireau, France, from 1694 to 1704, with Justice Hill and four gibbets in background.

With a population of 6,500 today, Condé-sur-Noireau is located about two hundred kilometres east of Paris, and thirty-three kilometres southwest of Caen, in Basse Normandie (Lower Normandy), in the department of Calvados. Still an industrial town, it produces primarily automotive equipment, books and magazines.[3]

On D-Day in 1944, the Allied forces (Britain, the Commonwealth, and the United States) began 98the invasion of France, to liberate it from German control. The Allies first landed on the beaches of Calvados northwest of Condé-sur-Noireau, destroying ninety-five percent of Condé with aerial bombs on their sweep toward Paris. The town's reconstruction was not completed until the inauguration of the city hall in 1963.

In my research I found a pen and ink sketch of Condé-sur-Noireau done in 1704, showing houses nestled in a valley with gentle hills rising in the background.[4] The dominant structure in the scene is the round chateau tower, built on a Roman foundation. Not far away is the dome-covered square tower of Saint Sauveur Church. This pastoral scene is rudely jarred by the four gibbets on the far Colline du Justice (Justice Hill) as identified at the bottom of the sketch.

Condé-sur-Noireau with Justice Hill in background, France, 2001.

A gibbet is a strong upright wooden post with one horizontal arm at the top. From that arm the corpse of an executed criminal was hung in an iron cage made to measure by a blacksmith. The gibbets were erected at prominent locations to deter crime.[5] The corpses were left to the elements, sometimes (especially if covered in tar) for years, to prevent relatives from taking them down for burial.

At Condé's city hall, I explained in fractured French and some English why I was there. At the mention of the name "Noget" one woman said there was a family by that name living on the outskirts of town, at an area called Vaux. We located an eager student at the tourist bureau who was most helpful—she even phoned the Noget family and told us we could meet them that afternoon. I was excited—would I find the missing link, the genealogical line back to Marie Anne?

We drove two kilometres to Vaux along a narrow country road to a T-junction surrounded by a smattering of farmhouses. Albert Noget and his wife came out to greet us. Albert, in his seventies, phoned his son André to come over with his wife and teenage daughter. (Albert and André are both dairy farmers whose products support the local cheese industry.) Somehow we managed to converse, but they did not know their genealogy—a disappointing dead end for my search.

City hall on left, beside the Druance River, Condé-sur-Noireau, France, 2001.

The only Nogets in the Roman Catholic cemetery were from the 1800s and later, and none in the adjacent smaller Protestant cemetery.

ST. HELIER, JERSEY, BRITISH CHANNEL ISLANDS

When I visited St. Helier with my husband in September 2001, we arrived by a ferry that whisked us sixty kilometres north from St. Malo in Brittany, France, in a mere seventy minutes. Quite a contrast to the long harrowing trip described by Louis over 260 years earlier.

In twentieth-century Jersey, English became the universal language, and the ancient dialect of Norman French nearly disappeared. It enjoyed a renaissance during the German occupation of World War Two, however. Because it is quite different from today's French, the Germans could not understand it, making Norman French the perfect medium of communication among locals in wartime. Today, islanders are dedicated to preserving the dialect.

I was eager to see Marie Anne and Louis' parish church and to soak up its atmosphere and history. Map in hand, we found our way to the corner of Bond and Mulcaster streets not far from the Royal Square.

1751 gold statue of King George II, Royal Square, St. Helier, Jersey, photo taken 2001.

While this location is central, the parish of St. Helier spreads far beyond the town.

I was thrilled to actually stand on the same stone floor they would have walked on for so many years for their weekly services and both happy and sad family events (their marriage, the baptisms of all seven children, and the burials of three of them). This was the only actual physical location (still standing) that I could connect with Marie Anne and Louis in my research.

Leaving the church, we glanced up to see the wooden statue of St. Helier the hermit as a robed monk gazing down at us from above the door inside the north porch. Martyred by decapitation from a Viking's axe, it was good to see him in one piece.

Seated on a park bench in Royal Square near the gilded statue of King George II, my husband and I enjoyed a picnic lunch in the shade of a chestnut tree. We tried to picture the area as a bustling market place in the 1700s, complete with sounds (lively chatter and bartering, perhaps the squeal of a pig that got loose), and smells (fish, rotting vegetables on the cobblestones, very fresh cattle manure). But the present was more prosaic: strutting pigeons and business people, laid-back shoppers and tourists, and even more-laid-back workmen on the scaffolding surrounding the Royal Court House. The golden king was not amused.

That afternoon of September 11, 2001, while we had been absorbed in eighteenth-century historical research at the Societé Jersiaise, almost three thousand innocent people were slaughtered. That figure was the total 1734 population of the parish of St. Helier. The purpose of our whole trip suddenly seemed insignificant.

LUNENBURG, NOVA SCOTIA

In 1995, Lunenburg's Old Town was awarded the title "World Heritage Site" by UNESCO (United Nations Educational, Scientific and Cultural Organization) in Paris. Since 1972 the list of sites has grown to include, among others: the Historic District of Quebec; Head-Smashed-In Buffalo Jump in Alberta; the Medieval City of Rhodes, Greece; the Taj Mahal in India; Stonehenge, England; and the Tower of London (built by William the Conqueror from Caen stone). Lunenburg is the best-preserved North American example of a British colonial town plan of the eighteenth century.

Louis Payzant's town lot was on Townshend Street, between Duke and King where the street dips just west of St. Andrew's Presbyterian Church (built in 1828). On our visit in 2002, a workman was removing white aluminum siding and black shutters, revealing the original

St. John's Anglican Church, Lunenburg, Nova Scotia, 1986.

Some remains of St. John's Anglican Church, Lunenburg, Nova Scotia, 2002.

beige shingle cladding. The owner had told him the house was about 225 years old (dating it to about 1777). Louis' town house on that very lot was likely built in 1753 for the first winter, but he may have moved to his island the next year.

In 1762, six years after Louis' death, the town house was still registered under the name "Luis Pesant." His eldest son, Philip, probably moved there in 1763 until he was able to have a house built on his three hundred-acre lot. Philip sold his father's town lot for the grand sum of £2 to the Reformed Congregation in January 1772. Soon after, the present two-storey Georgian house was likely built.

That house was no doubt remodelled in the mid-nineteenth century to add the distinctive "Lunenburg Bump" over the front door. This five-sided dormer window on the second floor extends out and down from the roof to create an overhang (over the front door) supported by two pillars that rest on the front stairs. There are many delightful variations of the Victorian "bump" on Lunenburg homes.

Louis' other Lunenburg properties were sold, but there is no trace of those transactions. In 1761 Marie Anne was given title to the thirty-acre lot (number four, Oakland, on Mahone Bay) and permission to sell it. At some point it was sold to Peter Zwicker by Zouberbuhler.[6]

Even though Louis' garden lot was registered to "Louis Paisang," it was listed as vacant in 1762 and supposedly reverted to the Crown. However, written opposite the statement is "Widow claims it."[7] Perhaps Marie Anne did get compensation.

Across the street from Louis' town lot, and to the west, is St. John's Anglican Church, or rather, what's left of it. Louis and Marie Anne were likely members of the church under the Reverend Jean Baptiste Moreau for the three years they lived in the community. Although considerably altered in the late nineteenth century, this white church with black trim (in the "Carpenter Gothic style") was Canada's second-oldest Protestant church, after St. Paul's in Halifax. Unfortunately, tragedy struck the church following a night of Halloween pranks in 2001, when arsonists torched it. Only charred remnants of the four walls remain. The local parishioners have promised to rebuild this National Historic Site, but sadly, it will never be the same.

The Star Fort, location of the early military barracks, is now gone, but on that hill stands the large, three-storey Lunenburg Academy. This National Historic Site, built in 1895, is painted white with black trim and topped with a red mansard roof. After a century, its walls still ring with the sound of children—it remains as a school.

The Eastern Blockhouse, where poor Jean Petrequin was kept captive in 1753, is gone as well, but it is remembered by "Blockhouse Hill" park, where the tourist bureau overlooks the town.

If Marie Anne and Louis were to visit today, the only thing they would recognize is the layout of the streets. Any traces of its origin as the Mi'kmaq and then Acadian settlement of Merligash and its rough beginning as a British settlement have disappeared.

COVEY'S ISLAND, MAHONE BAY, NOVA SCOTIA

In Nova Scotia's Mahone Bay where sailboats flock on sunny summer weekends, unspoiled Covey's Island (once known as Payzant's Island) is one of many that dot the area. It's hard to imagine the violent attack there in the spring of 1756.[8]

The island has been uninhabited for decades, but it was used commercially in the 1930s. In 1936 or earlier, Kentville financier George A. Chase bought Covey's Island in order to grow potatoes imported from Scotland or Northern Ireland (potatoes weren't allowed on the main-

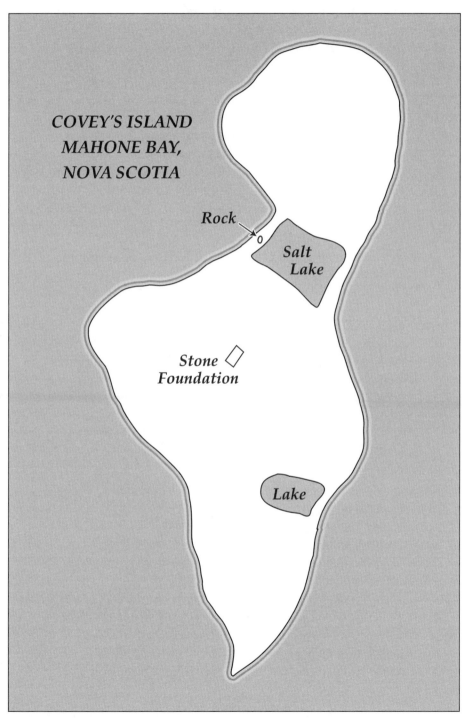

Map of Covey's Island, Mahone Bay, Nova Scotia.

land until they had been quarantined offshore for two years). Chase had a house built on the high hill, and a log cabin erected at the south end of Meisner's Cove. Parts of that cabin, logs greyed by the sun and wind, are still there today.

The 108-acre island, covered with meadows and woodlands, has two lakes: a large salt one in the flat area between the hills, and a small freshwater one. The latter, wrote Howard Jess who helped Chase, "was where we got our fresh water to spray our potatoes. Also we had three deer visit us when I was out there in 1938 and I saw them drinking water several times. It may be a little bit brackish at times when there is a strong wind from the north or north east that blows some surf on the lake. It sure was all fresh water when Louis Payzant settled there, because I would imagine some shore land has washed away over 230 years."[9]

After the quarantine, the crop was trucked to the Annapolis Valley for storage, and then planted on the North Mountain, near Kentville, in 1939. For several summers in the early 1940s, Robert Chase, the owner's cousin, took beef cattle to the island by scow for summer grazing. Howard Jess didn't know anyone else who had lived on the island since the potato summer of '37. In 1955 George A. Chase sold the island back to the Meisners.[10] Some of the locals still call it "Potato Island."

In 1986 a West German owned Covey's Island.[11] He was one of at least two thousand Germans who had bought cottage lots and small islands along Nova Scotia's six-thousand-kilometre coastline for about one tenth of what comparable vacation land would cost in Germany.[12]

The island was for sale in the spring of 2002 with a price tag of almost one million dollars. Rev. John Payzant would certainly raise an eyebrow if he knew, since he sold half of it for only £10 two hundred years before.

Families often picnic today at the sandy Meisner's Cove, on the west side of the uninhibited island. But lunch isn't the only reason they visit. Just beyond the beach towards the salt lake is an area of short, dense, green bushes. Through them, a worn pathway leads to a two-foot long rock, which appears to have a red handprint on it. There are no signs around, but everyone knows the story: it's Louis Payzant's "bloody handprint." For seven decades, maybe more, local people and those "from away" (usually Payzant descendants) have made the trip to see this unusual rock and recount the frightful scalping.

According to Nova Scotia folklorist Helen Creighton in 1950:

> [Louis] put his hand on the wound, which was bleeding freely, and then pressed it on a rock where the imprint still remains. At

Lewis King Payzant (1862–1946) and "Bloody Handprint" rock, Covey's Island, Nova Scotia, ca. 1937.

times it is seen clearly, a perfect impression of a man's hand with four fingers and thumb, and tinged with the red of blood. At other times the imprint seems to fade away. It has been the subject of much speculation ever since....Mr. Payzant was left with his hand upon the rock and it is thought that the heat from the fire burned the imprint indelibly.[13]

Stone foundation of house, Covey's Island, Nova Scotia, 2002.

The Nova Scotia Museum gives a scientific explanation. Most of the islands in Mahone Bay are drumlins, "or hills of glacially transported material dropped in their present position when the glaciers melted away 12,000 years ago." The rock is a boulder of the "Halifax Formation composed of altered slates [and] when close to a granite contact...develops a high pyrite (iron sulphide) composition. When pyrite weathers mostly by the action of a bacteria known as ferrobacillus thiobacillus, it generates new minerals [but only] in the proper conditions of humidity and temperature. Many of the new sulphate minerals created in this [way] change color [from] day to day.... Some are greenish-yellow and some are reddish-brown."[14]

In short, the museum explains that the handprint is merely reddish-brown mineral activity "along small eroded bedding planes," not human blood seared into the rock from the burning house. Even so, some locals call Covey's Island the "Island with the Bloody Hand."

On the hill south of the salt lake is a stone foundation. Robert

Cram, owner and restorer of Lunenburg's 1791 Lennox Inn, told me that this foundation could date from the eighteenth century. Dry-laid, the rubble boulders had been split vertically and placed with their flat sides facing the inside. Above ground, larger split-granite blocks sit upright on the boulders. The south wall has caved in toward the mound of grass on the bottom.

I stared at the foundation, wondering if this was the very site of the terrible raid so long ago. A house built here, well-sheltered from the north winds, would command an excellent view from this rise over-looking water to the east and west. The scorched ruins have long since returned to the earth, but after two-and-a-half centuries the stone foundation remains as mute evidence of the bloody raid.

MALISEET TREK—NOVA SCOTIA TO QUEBEC

The eighteenth-century route from Payzant's Island to Quebec City could possibly be canoed and portaged today, but personally, I prefer the comforts of a car.

Fort Edward (now a National Historic Site in Windsor, Nova Scotia) has all but disappeared today: only the wooden blockhouse and earthworks remain. The square blockhouse sits on a windy hill overlooking the St. Croix River to the east, and the Avon River (for-merly the Pisiquid River) to the west. They merge and flow into the Minas Basin. Here, at the junction of the two rivers, the average daily tidal fluctuation is twelve metres. When the Maliseet passed by carry-ing Marie Anne and the children, they must have timed their escape to take advantage of the tidal flows. Marie Anne couldn't have known that five years later she would spend the rest of her days in the Pisiquid area, within sight of Fort Edward.

The fort was first garrisoned by British troops during the Seven Years' War, then the American Revolution, and the War of 1812. By the 1870s most of the buildings within the palisade (soldiers' barracks, provision stores, magazine, kitchen, and brew house) had deteriorat-ed. The officers' barracks survived and was used as a quarantine hos-pital in World War One. Fire destroyed it in 1922.

In New Brunswick, the Petitcodiac River meanders through the city of Moncton, named after Lieutenant-Colonel Robert Monckton, whom Marie Anne and Louis might have met when he had been sent to Lunenburg to quell the 1753 insurrection. Not far from the city cen-tre, a twice-daily natural phenomenon occurs: the tidal bore. This twenty- to forty-five-centimetre-high, river-wide tidal wave runs north from the Bay of Fundy and rapidly fills the river basin. Within an hour the water level rises more than seven and a half metres.

Twelve hours later at low tide, the gulleys and banks of mudflats attract clouds of hungry birds. In 1756 the Maliseet would have paddled with the tide to the source of the Petitcodiac River and portaged to another that feeds into the Saint John River.

The route northwest from Fredericton to Quebec was called the "French Path," or "Temiscouata Trail."[15] Today the Trans-Canada Highway generally follows the same route alongside the Saint John River. As I drive there in the comfort of my car, I picture Marie Anne beside me on the water in a group of canoes. The wide placid river cuts a gentle swath through broad meadows that slope down to the shore. Marie Anne was probably in no mind to admire the area. Every paddle stroke would have reminded her of the loss of her husband and children.

Canoeing up the Saint John River, the Maliseet portaged around the large waterfalls, now Grand Falls, New Brunswick. It is here that the Maliseet legend of the maiden "Malabeam" was said to have occurred. Mohawks (the Maliseet's traditional enemies) took Malabeam captive after killing her husband and children. Forced to guide them on a raid against her people, Malabeam deliberately led them to their—and her own—death over the twenty-three-metre falls named Checanekepeag (The Destroying Giant).[16] It is said that her spirit may be seen in the mists at full moon. Marie Anne was a latter-day Malabeam, taken by canoe after witnessing her husband being killed and her children taken from her. But she would live and do everything in her power to get her children back.

QUEBEC CITY, QUEBEC

During a recent visit, my husband and I strolled along the ramparts that look southwest over the green Plains of Abraham and noticed some ten-year-old boys sprawled on their stomachs on the grassy width of the wall. They reminded us of John Payzant and his classmates watching bug-eyed at the battle before them, little realizing the impact of the outcome: North America would no longer be French-ruled.

Not far away is the Ursuline Convent. There, in 1759, Sister Esther Marie Joseph de l'Enfant Jesus (born Esther Wheelwright in Massachusetts and captured at the age of seven) eventually became the assistant superior, and in 1760 (after Marie Anne had returned to Nova Scotia), she was the first "English" superior of the Ursulines in Quebec.

At the Musée des Ursulines de Québec (Museum of the Quebec Ursulines) are displayed many artefacts such as birch bark embroidered boxes, hand-made lace, paintings, embroideries, and furniture. In the late 1980s, Montcalm's skull was displayed there in a glass case, but no longer. That skull and a leg bone were given an elaborate official funeral in October 2001. Those remains are now buried in the small Cimetière de l'Hôpital Général de Québec—Quebec's General Hospital Cemetery—in the Lower Town.

Much has been made of a possible connection between Marie Anne and Montcalm. For a story-writing contest in the 1880s, when interest in local history was high, a Payzant descendant wrote a short prize-winning fictional account of Marie Anne's life called "Troublesome Times."[17] The author claimed that Marie Anne was a sister of Montcalm but they were estranged because she, a Catholic, had married a Huguenot, "John Payzant" (this was an obvious error, as John was her son), without her parents' consent. The story also claimed that Montcalm wanted her brought to Quebec for her own safety during the Seven Years' War, so he sent friendly Indians to get her. After the story was published in the *Montreal Weekly Witness*, a flurry of letters to the editor pointed out the errors, but the deed was done. People believed it, and today descendants refuse to discount it.

The parents of the thirty-year-old author, Lucilla Payzant of Windsor Forks, Hants County, Nova Scotia, were both great grandchildren of Marie Anne and Louis through sons John and Lewis. Lucilla's father Joel was a well-travelled sailor who, "As an old man…was a brilliant storyteller at the fireside, delighting a wide-eyed audience of a rising generation with the tales of a world of long ago."[18] Lucilla's mother Caroline, however, wrote in 1894, "I am sorry to hear so many false statements concerning my ancestors."[19]

Lucilla later wrote that her source for the claim of a brother-sister relationship was "older members of the family…who suppose that she (Mary Payzant) was Montcalm's sister, and the story is told that at his death he sent for her and asked her forgiveness and she replied that she could forgive everything but the death of her husband. I do not know of any 'proof' to this, however."[20] The author admitted to inventing the early part of Marie Anne's life.

The facts are: Montcalm had three sisters, none named "Marie" or "Anne"; Marie Anne was born in 1711 in Normandy, not 1715 in Southern France; and Montcalm couldn't have ordered the May 8, 1756 Indian raid on Payzant's Island because he arrived at Quebec five days later. Neither John nor Lewis Payzant mentions Montcalm in their memoirs. The only references to him in other accounts appear after the 1880s.

Montcalm's original burial place, marked by a commemorative

plaque, is next door to the Musée des Ursulines de Québec in the ornate Ursuline Chapel, with its gilded sculpted décor. The chapel was restored in 1759 and several times since.

There is no record of Marie Anne or her girls having lived at the convent—she may never have lodged there at all.

Walking through iron gates next to the Notre Dame Basilica, we admired the Quebec seminary where John Payzant and his brothers may have lodged. Founded in 1633 by Bishop Laval, the seminary evolved into Laval University, moving southwest to suburban Ste-Foy in 1952.

To see a model of the town exactly as it was fifty years after Marie Anne lived in Quebec, we checked out the Model of Quebec inside the Interpretation Centre of the Artillery Park near the Saint John gate. It's interesting to note that the spacious formal gardens in the Upper Town have now been replaced with buildings.

The heart of the Lower Town is the cobblestoned Place Royale, the location of the old market and former site of Champlain's *abitation* (trading post). The Norman-style homes of merchants have been preserved virtually as they were in Marie Anne's time since their original walls were retained after the 1759 bombardment.

At the Saint Lawrence River, ferries dart back and forth to Lévis, a fifteen-minute trip. (British cannonballs were fired from there across to the Lower and Upper Towns in 1759.) Today tourists disembark from cruise ships at the dock to discover Old Quebec, starting from the Lower Town. From one of the docks, Marie Anne with her five children would have boarded a Halifax-bound ship in 1760, eager to leave the ruined town. I imagine her making one last turn glancing up at Quebec, marking the end of her four-year forced stay in the Roman Catholic capital of New France.

FALMOUTH, NOVA SCOTIA

The late historian John V. Duncanson (whose aunts and a cousin married Payzants) gave me a tour of Marie Anne's Falmouth. He was the first to tell me about Marie Anne's second husband. Even more exciting, he told me the identity of the man who murdered him. The murderer's children grew up to be very well-respected in the community, and his identity has therefore been kept quiet.

When John Duncanson was a boy in the 1920s and his grandparents owned the Payzant homestead, he recalled a visit from a very old man. "I...remember the visitor, a Mr. Payzant of Halifax or Dartmouth, NS, asking my grandfather for a section of any old apple tree which grew on the west side of the farm wood house. It was a

Depression in ground as evidence of Marie Anne Payzant's farmhouse, Falmouth, Nova Scotia, 2002.

Bow Sweet Apple tree and Mr. Payzant wanted to preserve the wood as a token from the Payzant farm."[21]

Not far from the site of the homestead is a spring-fed pond, known locally as "Marie Payzant's Soft Water Pond." Cattle used to water there. One woman recalls blocks of ice being cut from it in the winter for her mother's ice house in the 1920s.

A portion of Marie Anne's farm is now the Avon Valley Golf and Country Club. Established in 1971, it's a "challenging well-groomed 18 hole golf course" with "hilly terrain, prevailing winds and small greens."[22] At least modern suburbia hasn't spread over her original property—it's kept in pristine condition.

The former location of Marie Anne's log farmhouse is on the grounds of the country club. A depression in the ground behind the Pro Shop identifies the spot where it stood for over one hundred years. Probably built in the 1760s, it burned to the ground in the late 1800s, destroying valuable possessions and old records. A few brick fragments poke out of the grass, likely from the chimney.

Driving east from the golf club, Mr. Duncanson and I crossed the Alline Brook that runs down the hill from Davidson Lake to Pesaquid

Payzant monument, Falmouth Cemetery, Falmouth, Nova Scotia, 2002.

116   A Passion for Survival

Name from Payzant monument, Falmouth Cemetery, Falmouth, Nova Scotia, 2002.

Lake (the latter formed by the damming of the Avon River) across Marie Anne's original farm lot. Local tradition states that near this bridge, at the foot of Alline Hill, Peter Manning killed Malachi Caigin in 1776.[23] Golfers playing on the second hole know nothing of the murder committed near the brook over two hundred years ago.

The corner of Dyke Road and Town Road, now the site of Falmouth United Baptist Church, is the location of Marie Anne's first house, her town lot. She likely lived there in the "French house," an Acadian log home. On the church's corner lawn stands a stone memorial erected in 1984 to "Henry Alline 1748-1784." It reads: "A burning and shining light and justly acclaimed the apostle of Nova Scotia," referring to John Payzant's brother-in-law and friend.

Not far from the Baptist Church is the Falmouth Centre Cemetery. Originally called the "Old Burial Ground," it was part of the town plot laid out in 1760, near Fort Lawrence (which no longer exists). Legend states that in the late 1800s the remains from "Mount Piziquid" (the Payzant family burial ground on Marie Anne's farm lot, 400 metres north of her farmhouse[24]) were transferred to the cemetery, evidenced by depressions left on the farm site.[25]

The Falmouth Centre Cemetery is the last resting place for Marie Anne. A tall brick-red monument points skyward, commemorating four generations (nine Payzants)—from the progenitor Louis Payzant (circa 1695-1756) to his grandson's wife, Catherine Jane Payzant (1798-1870). It was probably erected after the death of Catherine Jane. The other family members who died earlier were likely transferred from Mount Piziquid. On one of the four sides of the monument is inscribed: "Lewis [Louis] Payzant died near Chester, N.S. He was the descendant of a Huguenot family [but he was a Huguenot] who fled from France on the Revocation of the Edict of Nantes [well, fifty-four years later, at the age of forty-four]. Also Mary, his wife. The above were the grandparents of Peter Payzant." Those Payzants listed on the monument are: Marie Anne and Louis, Lewis and Grace, Peter and Catherine Jane, and three young children of the latter.

Many people in the Falmouth area trace their ancestry back to three of Marie Anne and Louis' children—Lewis, Lisette, and John. Although John moved to Liverpool, one of his sons returned to Falmouth. I'm descended from him, Rev. William Payzant (1782-1868), through his son William Henry Payzant (1827-1885), and his son A.D. Payzant (1868-1945), and his daughter Mary Layton (née Payzant, 1916-).

I wish I could chat over a cup of tea with an elderly Marie Anne in Falmouth and hear her French-accented voice recount her memorable life.

She might gaze through the window at the sun on her garden and reminisce of her happy and innocent childhood in Condé-sur-Noireau—how she'd love to run up the surrounding hills and look down at the village houses around the chateau tower and watch the birds dart in and out of their pigeon house. But a frown would cloud her face as she tells me about her escape from France and the last time she saw her Condé.

Tilting her head and tracing the handle of her cup, she smiles as she describes her marriage to the handsome Louis in St. Helier parish church, and how she loved those silver wedding shoes. A tear rolls down her cheek as she remembers little Jean Louis, Marie and Anne who were taken by God too early.

With her hand on her stomach she rolls her eyes and feigns the seasickness that she and the children suffered for the first few weeks of their Atlantic journey—it never bothered Louis. She recalls the frightening night of the Lunenburg insurrection and later the utter joy on Louis' face as he played king of his own island. He had great plans for a business in Lunenburg, and for their child of the new land.

She starts to sob and reverts to French. Their world and future plans had been shattered in a matter of minutes. I leave her for a while and walk to the window—clouds have begun to roll in from the Avon River. Regaining her composure, Marie Anne says she'd rather not describe the Indian raid or the arduous trek through Acadia to Quebec—it's too painful.

Her face lights up again as she calls to mind the day her children were reunited with her in Quebec. Though they were ragged, she recognized them at once. They had been well-cared for, but ten-year-old Philip was a changed boy. She always worried about him. The only comment she makes about her four years in Quebec was how she longed for the day she could leave as a free woman.

As she speaks about Malachi Caigin she brushes the air with her hands. She certainly didn't love him, but he was a help when she needed it. No, Louis was the love of her life.

She smiles as the sun breaks through the clouds and fills the room with warmth. She's proud of her children, who overcame tragedy, married, and were living full lives. Her son Lewis has been good to her.

I wish I could tell her what happened to her children and grandchildren—she'd love to know. She would be amazed to learn she has thousands of descendants in North America. She lived through so many trials and heartaches, but she survived. Louis would be proud of her.

Endnotes

PREFACE – THROUGH THE TINTYPE

1   Marion M. Payzant, *The Payzant and Allied Jess and Juhan Families in North America* (Wollaston, Mass.: n.p., 1970).

2   Joyce Barkhouse, "Massacre at Mahone Bay," *Canadian Frontier* (Langley, B.C.: Garnet Publishing, 1974), Vol. 3, No. 2.

3   Linda G. Wood, "The Lunenburg Indian Raids of 1756 and 1758: A New Documentary Source," *Nova Scotia Historical Review* (Halifax, N.S.: Public Archives of Nova Scotia, 1993), Vol. 13, No. 1, p. 93.

4   Miscellaneous Manuscripts Collection, Nova Scotia Archives and Records Management (NSARM), MG100, Vol. 263, No. 1.

5   Mary N. Layton to Linda G. Layton, April 2002.

6   Paroisse de St. Helier, Registre des Mariages et Enterrements 1719–1750, p. 48. Jersey Archive reference G/C/03/A1/4, Jersey, Channel Islands.

7   Crown Land Grants, NSARM, Old Book 4, p. 114 (mfm).

8   Archibald MacMechan, "The Payzant Captivity," *The Sunday Leader* (Halifax, N.S.: n.p., 20 February 1921).

9   B.C. Cuthbertson, "Payzant, John," *Dictionary of Canadian Biography* (Toronto: University of Toronto Press, 1979), Vol. VI, p. 573.

10 Abjuration de Anne Noget, 8 décembre 1756, Registre des Abjurations, Archives de l'Archidiocèse de Québec, AAQ, 66 CD, Vol. A:74.

11 Webster's *Ninth New Collegiate Dictionary* (Markham, Ont.: Thomas Allen & Son, 1984), p. 866.

12 Payzant, *The Payzant Families*, p. v.

13 Ibid. p. vi.

14 Marion M. Payzant, *A Scrapbook with Notes on the Payzant and Allied Jess and Juhan*

Families in North America ([Wollaston, Mass.]: n.p., 1961–1963) Vol. 1, p. 4.

15 Louis Paysant to De Vastan, 20 March 1738, Archives départementales du Calvados, Caen, France, 1 B 2.199, dossier Paysant.

16 Louis Paysant to De Launay, 19 September 1739, Archives départementales du Calvados, Caen, France, 1 B 2.199, dossier Paysant.

17 Anne Osselin to Linda G. Layton, 18 March 2002.

18 Dossier Paysant, Archives départementales du Calvados, Caen, France, 1 B 2.199.

19 Paroisse de St. Helier, Registre. Also, Payzant, *The Payzant Families*, p. xxv.

20 Miscellaneous Manuscripts Collection, NSARM, MG100, Vol. 263, No. 1.

21 Abjuration de Anne Noget.

22 Baptême de Louise Catherine Paisant, 27 décembre 1756, Registre de l'état civil de Notre-Dame-de-Québec, CN301, S1/36, p. 91, verso, Archives nationales du Québec, Saint-Foy, Québec.

23 Brian C. Cuthbertson, ed., *The Journal of the Reverend John Payzant* (1749–1834), (Hantsport, N.S.: Lancelot Press, 1981).

24 Silas Tertius Rand, "Early Provincial Settlers," *The Provincial* (Halifax, N.S.: n.p., August 1852) Vol. 1, No. 8.

25 Payzant family papers, NSARM, MG1, Vol. 747, No. 42.

CHAPTER ONE – LOUIS IN CAEN (CA. 1695–1739)

1 Elizabeth Gaskell, *Traits and Stories of the Huguenots* <www.lang.nagoya-u.ac.jp/~matsuoka/EG-Traits.html>, 1997. Written in 1853.

2 R.R. Palmer, *A History of the Modern World* (New York: Alfred A. Knopf, 1964), pp. 74–76, 115–116.

3 Samuel Smiles, *The Huguenots: Their Settlements, Churches and Industries in England and Ireland* (London: John Murray, 1905), p. 156.

4 Ibid.

5 Paul Jubert, "Louis Paisant, Religionnaire et Fugitif," *Bulletin de la Société des Antiquaries de Normandie* (Caen, France: La Société, 1961–62), Tome 56, pp. 620–633. Also microfilmed by the Genealogical Society of the Church of Jesus Christ of Latter-Day Saints, 23 February 1965.

6 Smiles, *The Huguenots*, p. 149.

7 G.A. Rothrock, *The Huguenots: A Biography of a Minority* (Chicago: Nelson-Hall, 1979), p. 172.

8 Charles W. Baird, History of the Huguenot Emigration to America (Baltimore: Genealogical Publishing, 1973), Vol. 2, p. 67. Originally published in 1885.

9 Smiles, *The Huguenots*, p. 166.

10 Ibid. p. 169.

11 Ibid.

12 Ibid. p. 168.

13 *The Quiet Conquest: The Huguenots 1685–1985* (London: Museum of London, 1985), p. 44.

14 Huguenot Society of South Africa, *The Méreau*, <www.geocities.com/Heartland/Valley/8140/mer-e.htm>.

15 Will and Ariel Durant, *The Age of Voltaire* (New York: Simon & Schuster, 1965), p. 727.

16 The Clio Collective, *Quebec Women: A History* (Toronto: Women's Press, 1987), p. 66.

17 Jubert, "Louis Paisant."

18 Brian C. Cuthbertson, ed., *The Journal of the Reverend John Payzant* (1749–1834), (Hantsport, N.S.: Lancelot Press, 1981), p. 15.

19 Stuart A. Kallen, ed., *The 1700s: Headlines in History* (San Diego, Calif.: Greenhaven Press, 2001).

20 Marion M. Payzant, *The Payzant and Allied Jess and Juhan Families in North America* (Wollaston, Mass.: n.p., 1970), p. x.

21 Abbé Louis Huet, *Histoire de Condé-sur-Noireau: Ses Seigneurs, Son Industrie, etc.* (Caen: F. Le Blanc-Hardel, 1883), p. 185. Also microfilmed by the Genealogical Society of the Church of Jesus Christ of Latter-Day Saints, 1964.

22 Louis Ducros, *French Society in the Eighteenth Century* (London: G. Bell & Sons, 1926), p. 215.

23 Jubert, "Louis Paisant."

24 Louis Paysant to De Vastan, 20 March 1738, Archives départementales du Calvados, Caen, France, 1 B 2.199, dossier Paysant.

25 Ibid.

26 Ibid.

27 Ibid.

28 Pierre Jacques Guerard, Request to Le Courtois, August 1741, Archives départementales du Calvados, Caen, France, 1 B 2.199, dossier Paysant.

29 Louis Paysant to Pierre Lieux, 19 September 1739, Archives départementales du Calvados, Caen, France, 1 B 2.199, dossier Paysant. Louis said he had paid her "until last St. Clair." July 16 is the feast day for St. Clair, an English-born French hermit and martyr, famous for his healing abilities, who was murdered in 884 at St. Clair-sur-Epte, northwest of Paris.

30 Smiles, *The Huguenots*, p. 163.

31 Gaskell, *Traits*.

32 Smiles, *The Huguenots*, p. 174.

33 Ibid. p. 163.

34 Louis Paysant to Gosset, 19 September 1739, Archives départementales du Calvados, Caen, France, 1 B 2.199, dossier Paysant.

35 *The First Canadian Library: the Library of the Jesuit College of New France*, 1632–1800 (Ottawa: National Library of Canada, 1972), p. 14.

36 Jubert, "Louis Paisant."

37 Le Courtois, Prosecution Address, December 1739, Archives départementales du Calvados, Caen, France, 1 B 2.199, dossier Paysant.

38 Le Senecal, Summons, 12 December 1739, Archives départementales du Calvados, Caen, France, 1 B 2.199, dossier Paysant.

39 Dumorestier, Sale of Louis Paysant's Estate, December 1741 Archives départementales du Calvados, Caen, France, 1 B 2.199, dossier Paysant.

40 Jubert, "Louis Paisant."

CHAPTER TWO – JERSEY, ISLAND OF REFUGE (1739–1753)

1 Louis Paysant to Pierre Lieux, 19 September 1739, Archives départementales du Calvados, Caen, France, 1 B 2.199, dossier Paysant.

2 Louis Paysant to Gosset, 19 September 1739, Archives départementales du Calvados, Caen, France, 1 B 2.199, dossier Paysant.

3 Edmund Toulmin Nicolle, *The Town of St. Helier, its Rise and Development* (Jersey, Channel Isles: Bigwood, 1931), p. 64. Originally from Falle's History of Jersey, 2nd ed., 1734.

4 Joseph R. Smallwood, ed. in chief, "Channel Islands," *Encyclopedia of Newfoundland and Labrador* (N.p. : Newfoundland Book Pub. (1967) Ltd., 1981) Vol. 1, p. 400.

5 Smallwood, ed. in chief, "Fisheries," *Encyclopedia of Newfoundland and Labrador,* Vol. 1, p. 130.

6 Louis Paysant to Pierre Lieux, 19 September 1739.

7 Marie-Louis Backhurst to Linda G. Wood, 28 November 1986.

8 Abjuration de Anne Noget, 8 décembre 1756, Registre des Abjurations, Archives de l'Archidiocise de Québec, AAQ, 66 CD, Vol. A:74.

9 Brian C. Cuthbertson, ed., *The Journal of the Reverend John Payzant* (1749-1834) (Hantsport, N.S.: Lancelot Press, 1981) p. 15.

10 Camille Cautru, *L'Histoire de Condé-sur-Noireau* (Condé-sur-Noireau: Corlet, 196?) p. 11.

11 Ibid. p. 141.

12 Ibid. p. 135.

13 Ibid. p. 144.

14 Paul Jubert, "Louis Paisant, Religionnaire et Fugitif," *Bulletin de la Société des Antiquaries de Normandie* (Caen, France: La Société, 1961–62) Tome 56, 620–633. Also microfilmed by the Genealogical Society of the Church of Latter-Day Saints, 23 February 1965. In 1960 Paul Jubert of Caen, France, researched the Payzant family for the American genealogist Marion M. Payzant. As a result of his research, he wrote this in-depth paper.

15 Abbé Louis Huet, *Histoire de Condé-sur-Noireau: Ses Seigneurs, Son Industrie, etc.* (Caen: F. Le Blanc-Hardel, 1883), p. 307. Also microfilmed by the Genealogical Society of the Church of Jesus Christ of Latter-Day Saints, 1964.

16 Anne Osselin to Linda G. Wood, 4 June 1991. From A. Galland, *Histoire du protestantisme á Caen et en Basse-Normandie* (N.p.: n.p., 1898), found at the Bibliothèque protestante in Paris (B.S.H.P.F. No. 2924).

17 Anne Osselin to Linda G. Wood, 4 June 1991. From A. LeBoitteux, *Les Huguenots des Isles—Histoire de l'Église Reformée de Condé-sur-Noireau*, 1555–1685 (N.p.: n.p., 1906), found at the Bibliothèque protestante in Paris (B.S.H.P.F. No. 14584).

18 Ibid.

19 Anne Osselin to Linda G. Wood, 4 June 1991. From A. Galland, *Le Protestantisme á Condé-sur-Noireau* (N.p.: n.p., 1900?).

20 Ibid.

21 Paroisse de St. Helier, Registre des Mariages et Enterrements 1719–1750, p. 48. Jersey Archive reference G/C/03/A1/4, Jersey, Channel Islands.

22 Marion M. Payzant, *The Payzant and Allied Jess and Juhan Families in North America* (Wollaston, Mass.: n.p., 1970), p. 189.

23 Francis Corbet, *The Parish Church of Saint Helier*, Jersey ([St. Helier, Jersey: n.p., 1993]), p. 9.

24 Louis Payzant to James Payzant, 25 October 1742, Public Record Office, London, England, State Papers 36/59 pt. 2, folio 168.

25 Nicolle, *The Town*, p. 71.

26 Nicolle, *The Town*, p. 51.

27 Nicolle, *The Town*, p. 50.

28 Balleine's *History of Jersey*, rev. ed. (Chichester, West Sussex: Phillimore, 1998), p. 189.

29 Winthrop Pickard Bell, *The "Foreign Protestants" and the Settlement of Nova Scotia*, 2nd ed. ([Sackville, N.B.]: Mount Allison University, 1990), p. 131.

30 Bell, *Foreign Protestants*, p. 9.

31 Cuthbertson, ed., *The Journal*, p. 15.

32 Shipping Returns 1753–1757, NSARM, C.O.221, Vol. 28, p. 228 (mfm).

33 Mather Byles DesBrisay, *History of the County of Lunenburg* (Belleville, Ont.: Mika Publishing, 1972), p. 498. Written in 1870.

34 Shipping Returns 1753–1757, NSARM, C.O.221, Vol. 28, p. 236 (mfm).

CHAPTER THREE – LUNENBURG, A NEW BEGINNING (1753–1756)

1 Winthrop Pickard Bell, The *"Foreign Protestants" and the Settlement of Nova Scotia*, 2nd ed. ([Sackville, N.B.]: Mount Allison University, 1990), p. 13.

2 J. Murray Beck, "Cornwallis, Edward," *Dictionary of Canadian Biography* (Toronto: University of Toronto Press, 1979) Vol. IV, p. 168.

3 P.B. Waite, ed., *Pre-Confederation* (Scarborough, Ont.: Prentice-Hall, 1965) Vol. 2, p. 12. Cornwallis to Duke of Bedford, 23 July 1749.

4 Bell, *Foreign Protestants*, p. 344.

5 Ibid. p. 130.

6   Public Archives of Nova Scotia, "Lunenburg, Lunenburg County," *Place-Names and Places of Nova Scotia* (Belleville, Ont.: Mika Publishing, 1982).

7   Bell, *Foreign Protestants*, p. 406.

8   Ibid. p. 419.

9   William Cotterell to John Pownall, 30 July 1753. NSARM, RG1, Vol. 38A, p. 87.

10 Shipping Returns, 1753-1757, NSARM, C.O. 221, Vol. 28, p. 255 (mfm).

11 Joseph R. Smallwood, ed. in chief, "Fisheries," *Encyclopedia of Newfoundland and Labrador* (N.p. : Newfoundland Book Pub. (1967) Ltd., 1981) Vol. 1, p. 130.

12 Bell, *Foreign Protestants*, p. 409.

13 Charles Lawrence, *Journal and Letters of Col. Charles Lawrence*, NSARM, F90 N85 AR2b, p. 42.

14 Bell, *Foreign Protestants*, p. 411.

15 Ibid. p. 437.

16 Ibid. p. 204.

17 Ibid. p. 455.

18 "Foreign Protestants" card index, Winthrop Bell papers, NSARM, MG1, Vol. 122.

19 Bell, *Foreign Protestants*, 439.

20 Ibid. p. 439.

21 Ibid. p. 410.

22 Lunenburg County Land Grants, NSARM, RG20, "C," Vol. 90A, doc. 22.

23 Crown Land Grants, NSARM, Old Book 4, p. 114 (mfm).

CHAPTER FOUR – ISLAND ATTACK (1756)

1   "Foreign Protestants" card index, Winthrop Bell papers, NSARM, MG1, Vol. 122.

2   Winthrop Pickard Bell, The *"Foreign Protestants" and the Settlement of Nova Scotia*, 2nd ed. ([Sackville, N.B.]: Mount Allison University, 1990), p. 505.

3   Silas Tertius Rand, "Early Provincial Settlers," *The Provincial* (Halifax, N.S.: n.p., August 1852), Vol. I, No. 8, p. 301.

4   Brian C. Cuthbertson, ed., *The Journal of the Reverend John Payzant (1749–1834)* (Hantsport, N.S.: Lancelot Press, 1981), p. 15.

5   Ibid.

6   Rand, "Early Settlers," p. 302.

7   Jacques Lacoursière, Jean Provencher, Denis Vaugeois, *Canada-Québec: Synthèse Historique 1534–2000* (Sillery, Qué.: Septentrion, 2000), p. 105.

8   Payzant family papers, NSARM, MG1, Vol. 747, No.42.

9   *Cutting to the Chase of a Long-time Debate*, <www.mze.com/ sunshineparty/scalping.html>.

10 Stanley Pargellis, *Military Affairs in North America, 1748–1765* (Hamden, CT: Archon Books, 1969), p. 189.

11 J.C.B., *Travels in New France*, Sylvester K. Stevens et al., eds. (Harrisburg: The Pennsylvania Historical Commission, 1941), pp. 67–68. "J.C.B." was a French soldier.

12 Rand, *"Early Settlers,"* p. 303.

13 Ibid.

14 Don Gillmor and Pierre Turgeon, *Canada: A People's History, Volume One* (Toronto: McClelland & Stewart, 2000), p. 92.

15 Emma Lewis Coleman, *New England Captives Carried to Canada Between 1677 and 1760 During the French and Indian Wars* (Portland, Maine: Southworth Press, 1925), Vol. 2.

16 Gérard Finn, "Le Loutre, Jean-Louis," *Dictionary of Canadian Biography* (Toronto: University of Toronto Press, 1979), Vol. IV, p. 457.

17 Peter L. McCreath and John G. Leefe, *A History of Early Nova Scotia* (Tantallon, N.S.: Four East Publications, 1982).

18 Coleman, *New England Captives*, Vol. 2, p. 410.

19 Gillmor and Turgeon, *Canada*, p. 104. Written by Marquis de la Jonquiere, Governor of New France, 1749–1752.

20 Guy Frégault, *Canada: The War of the Conquest* (Toronto: Oxford University Press, 1969), p. 120. Written by Vaudreuil, 8 June 1756.

21 John Demos, *The Unredeemed Captive: a Family Story from Early America* (New York: Knopf, 1994), p. 133.

22 W.J. Eccles, "Seven Years' War," *The Canadian Encyclopedia* (Edmonton: Hurtig Publishers, 1985), p. 1680.

23 Pierre-François de Rigaud, Marquis de Vaudreuil, "Lettre de Vaudreuil au Ministre, Montréal, le 6 aôut 1756," *Public Archives of Canada Report for 1905* (Ottawa: Public Archives of Canada, 1905), Vol. II, App. A, Part III, p. 181.

24 Linda G. Wood, "The Lunenburg Indian Raids of 1756 and 1758: A New Documentary Source," *Nova Scotia Historical Review* (Halifax, N.S.: Public Archives of Nova Scotia, 1993), Vol. 13, No. 1, p. 93.

25 Miscellaneous Manuscripts Collection, NSARM, MG100, Vol. 263, No. 1.

26 Nova Scotia Council, minutes of meetings, 1753–1757, NSARM, RG1, Vol. 210.

27 Ibid.

28 Churches—Lunenburg—St. Johns, NSARM, book 1, burials 1752–1787 (mfm).

29 Helen Creighton, *Folklore of Lunenburg County, Nova Scotia* (Toronto: McGraw-Hill Ryerson Ltd., 1950), p. 146.

30 Vaudreuil, p. 181.

31 Rand, "Early Settlers," p. 302.

32 Licence to dispose of lands, NSARM, RG1, Vol. 165, No.175, and Crown Land Grants, NSARM, Old Book 4, p. 114 (mfm).

33 Lunenburg County Deeds, NSARM, Vol. 10, No. 48, p. 33 (mfm).

34 Mather Byles DesBrisay, *History of the County of Lunenburg* (Belleville, Ont.: Mika

Publishing, 1972), p. 501. Written in 1870.

35 Marion M. Payzant, *A Scrapbook with Notes on the Payzant and Allied Jess and Juhan Families in North America* ([Wollaston, Mass.]: n.p., 1961–63), Vol. IV.

CHAPTER FIVE – MALISEET TREK (1756)

1 Silas Tertius Rand, "Early Provincial Settlers," *The Provincial* (Halifax, N.S.: n.p., August 1852), Vol. I, No. 8, p. 303.

2 Payzant family papers, NSARM, MG1, Vol. 747, No.42. As told in 1860 by Elias Payzant (1778–1870), son of Louis Payzant (1751–1845).

3 William Pope, *Portrait of Windsor* (Windsor, N.S.: Lancelot Press, 1974).

4 John V. Duncanson, *Township of Falmouth, Nova Scotia* (Belleville, Ont.: Mika Publishing., 1983), p. 4.

5 Ibid. p. 7.

6 Rand, "Early Settlers," p. 304.

7 Abraham Gesner, *New Brunswick* (London: Simmonds & Ward, 1847), p. 108.

8 Geographic Board of Canada, *Handbook of Indians of Canada*, (Toronto: Coles, 1971), p. 78. Written in 1913.

9 Ibid.

10 Payzant family papers, NSARM.

11 Rand, "Early Settlers," p. 304.

12 Ibid.

13 Payzant family papers, NSARM.

14 J.C.B., *Travels in New France*, Sylvester K. Stevens et al., eds. (Harrisburg: The Pennsylvania Historical Commission, 1941), pp. 67–68. "J.C.B." was a French soldier. Written between 1757 and 1759.

15 John Witherspoon, "Journal of John Witherspoon," *Collections of the Nova Scotia Historical Society 1878–1884* (Belleville, Ont.: Mika Publishing, 1976) Vol. II, pp. 31–33.

16 Father Antoine Silvy, S.J., *Letters from North America* (Belleville, Ont.: Mika Publishing, 1980), p. 132. Written in 1709.

17 Esther Clark Wright, *The Saint John River and its Tributaries* (Wolfville, N.S.: n.p., 1966), p. 152.

18 Micheline D. Johnson, "Germain, Charles" *Dictionary of Canadian Biography* (Toronto: University of Toronto Press, 1979), Vol. IV, pp. 289–290.

19 J. Clarence Webster, ed., *Memorial on Behalf of the Sieur de Boishébert* (Saint John, N.B.: New Brunswick Museum, 1942), p. 14. Written in 1763.

20 Phyllis E. LeBlanc, "Deschamps de Boishébert et de Raffetot, Charles," *Dictionary of Canadian Biography* (Toronto: University of Toronto Press, 1979), Vol. IV, p. 214.

21 Emma Lewis Coleman, *New England Captives Carried to Canada Between 1677 and 1760 During the French and Indian Wars* (Portland, Maine: Southworth Press, 1925), Vol. 1,p. 45.

22 Rand, "Early Settlers," p. 304.

23 Payzant family papers, NSARM.

24 Vincent O. Erickson, "Maliseet," *Encyclopedia of World Cultures, Vol. I, North America* (Boston: G.K. Hall, 1991), p. 210.

25 Ibid. p. 210.

26 Silvy, S.J., *Letters*, p. 115.

27 Erickson, "Maliseet," p. 212.

28 Brian C. Cuthbertson, ed., *The Journal of the Reverend John Payzant (1749–1834)* (Hantsport, N.S.: Lancelot Press, 1981), p. 16.

CHAPTER SIX – QUEBEC CAPTIVITY (1756–1760)

1 Stuart Trueman, *An Intimate History of New Brunswick* (Toronto: McClelland & Stewart, 1970). A 1788 mid-winter snowshoe trip from Fredericton to Quebec (around 400 miles) took nine days.

2 Laurier L. LaPierre, *1759: The Battle for Canada* (Toronto: McClelland & Stewart, 1990), p. 114.

3 J.H. Stewart Reid, Kenneth McNaught, Harry S. Crowe, eds. *A Source-book of Canadian History: Selected Documents and Personal Papers* (Toronto: Longmans, 1964), p. 17. Written by Peter Kalm, 1749.

4 Ibid.

5 Reid, *Source-book*, 42. Written by General James Murray, 1762.

6 LaPierre, *1759*, p. 50.

7 G. Elmore Reaman, *The Trail of the Huguenots in Europe, the United States, South Africa and Canada* (Toronto: Thomas Allen, 1963), p. 201.

8 Gordon Donaldson, *Battle for a Continent, Quebec 1759* (Toronto: Doubleday, 1973), p. 51.

9 Clio Collective, *Quebec Women: a History* (Toronto: The Women's Press, 1987), p. 62.

10 John Demos, *The Unredeemed Captive: a Family Story from Early America* (New York: Knopf, 1994), p. 78.

11 Silas Tertius Rand, "Early Provincial Settlers," *The Provincial* (Halifax: n.p., August 1852), Vol. I, No. 8, p. 305.

12 Clio Collective, *Quebec Women*.

13 Canadian Museum of Civilization Corp., *Museum of New France, Schools in New France*, <www.civilization.ca/vmnf/education/eco00_e.html>, 2002

14 Gabrielle Lapointe, "Migeon de Branssat (Bransac), Marie-Anne, dite de la Nativité," *Dictionary of Canadian Biography* (Toronto: University of Toronto Press, 1979), Vol. IV, p. 535.

15 Gerald M. Kelly, "Wheelwright, Esther (rebaptized Marie-Joseph), dite de l'Enfant-Jésus," *Dictionary of Canadian Biography* (Toronto: University of Toronto Press, 1979), Vol. IV, p. 764.

16 Emma Lewis Coleman, *New England Captives Carried to Canada Between 1677 and*

1760 During the French and Indians Wars (Portland, Maine: Southworth Press, 1925), Vol. II, p. 429.

17 Coleman, *New England Captives*, p. 431.

18 Rand, "Early Settlers," p. 305.

19 Jean-Guy Lavalée, "Dubreil de Pontbriand, Henri-Marie," *Dictionary of Canadian Biography* (Toronto: University of Toronto Press, 1974), Vol. III, p. 193.

20 Abjuration de Anne Noget, 8 décembre 1756, Registre des Abjurations, Archives de l'Archidiocise de Québec, AAQ, 66CD, Vol. A:74.

21 Coleman, *New England Captives*, Vol. II, p. 410.

22 Pierre Lafontaine (Archiviste auxiliaire, Archives de l'Archidiocèse de Québec) to Linda G. Layton, 19 August 2002.

23 J.F. Bosher, *Men and Ships in the Canada Trade, 1660–1760: a Biographical Dictionary* (Ottawa: National Historic Sites, Environment Canada, 1992), p. 18.

24 L'Abbé Cyprien Tanguay, *Dictionnaire Généalogique des Families Canadiennes* (Montréal: Éditions Elysée, 1975). Written in 1889.

25 Jean-Pierre Asselin, "Récher, Jean-Félix," *Dictionary of Canadian Biography* (Toronto: University of Toronto Press, 1974), Vol. III, p. 545.

26 Baptême de Louise Catherine Paisant 27 décembre 1756, Registre de l'état de Notre-Dame-de-Québec, CN301, S1/36, 91, verso, Archives nationales du Québec, Saint-Foy, Québec.

27 Armand Gagne (Archiviste, Archives de l'Archidiocèse de Québec) to Linda G. Wood, 25 September 1989.

28 Lafontaine to Layton.

29 Tanguay, *Dictionnaire Généalogique.*

30 Payzant family papers, NSARM, MG1, Vol. 747, No. 42.

31 Rand, "Early Settlers," p. 305.

32 Marion M. Payzant, *A Scrapbook with Notes on the Payzant and Allied Jess and Juhan Families in North America* ([Wollaston, Mass.]: n.p., 1961–63). Written by Nellie May Young, 1962.

33 Brian C. Cuthbertson, ed., *The Journal of the Reverend John Payzant (1749–1834)* (Hantsport, N.S.: Lancelot Press, 1981), p. 17.

34 André Vachon, *Taking Root: Canada from 1700 to 1760* (Ottawa: Public Archives of Canada, 1985), p. 246.

35 Père Joseph Cosette (Archiviste, Archives de la Compagnie de Jésus, Saint-Jerome, Qué.) to Linda G. Wood, 31 August 1987.

36 Payzant family papers, NSARM.

37 Cuthberton, ed., *The Journal*, p. 16.

38 LaPierre, *1759*, p. 126.

39 George F.G. Stanley, *New France, the Last Phase 1744–60* (Toronto: McClelland & Stewart, 1968), p. 194.

40 Henri Têtu, "M. Jean-Félix Récher, Curé de Québec, et Son Journal 1757–1760,"

Bulletin des Recherches Historiques (Québec: n.p., 1903) Vol. 9, No. 10, p. 292. Written 28 June 1757.

41 Ibid. p. 296. Written 29 July 1757.

42 Ibid. p. 299. Written 31 August 1757.

43 Ibid. p. 306. Written 12 May 1758.

44 LaPierre, *1759*, p. 134.

45 Payzant family papers, NSARM.

46 Lapointe, "Migeon de Branssat (Bransac)," p. 535.

47 LaPierre, *1759*, p. 141.

48 LaPierre, *1759*, p. 256.

49 Rand, "Early Settlers," p. 301.

50 Lapointe, "Migeon de Branssat (Bransac)," p. 535.

51 Gordon Donaldson, *Battle for a Continent, Quebec 1759* (Toronto: Doubleday, 1973), p. 207.

52 Asselin, "M. Jean-Félix Récher," p. 547.

53 Payzant, *A Scrapbook*, Vol. I. Also "Peonett," Vol. II, p. 90.

CHAPTER SEVEN – FALMOUTH, ANOTHER BEGINNING (1761–1796)

1 Marion M. Payzant, *A Scrapbook with Notes on the Payzant and Allied Jess and Juhan Families in North America* ([Wollaston, Mass.]: n.p., 1961–63), Vol. 1. The author devotes many pages of genealogy to the Perrotte family of Caen, France (the same name as the merchant who rented Louis' shop when he fled in 1739). However, according to the Liverpool Records (Vol. II, 90) in this scrapbook, the name was "Peonett."

2 John V. Duncanson, *Township of Falmouth, Nova Scotia*, (Belleville, Ont.: Mika Publishing, 1983), p. 11.

3 Winthrop Pickard Bell, The *"Foreign Protestants" and the Settlement of Nova Scotia*, 2nd ed. ([Sackville,N.B.]: Mount Allison University, 1990), p. 340.

4 Marion M. Payzant, *The Payzant and Allied Jess and Juhan Families in North America* (Wollaston, Mass.: n.p., 1970), p. 189.

5 Duncanson, *Township of Falmouth*, p. 17.

6 Payzant, *Payzant Families*, p. xiii.

7 Crown Land Grants, NSARM, Old Book 4, p. 114 (mfm).

8 Licence to dispose of lands, NSARM, RG1, Vol. 165, No.175.

9 Payzant, *Payzant Families*, p. 189.

10 Payzant family papers, NSARM, MG1, Vol. 747, No. 42.

11 Linda G. Wood, "Murder Among the Planters: A Profile of Malachi Caigin of Falmouth, Nova Scotia," *Nova Scotia Historical Review* (Halifax, N.S.: Public Archives of Nova Scotia, 1996), Vol. 16, No. 1, p. 96.

12 Chipman Family Papers, NSARM, MG1, Vol. 181, No. 11.

13 Ibid. No. 13.

14 Falmouth Township Book 1748–1825, NSARM, MG4, Vol. 31B (mfm.).

15 Chipman Family Papers, NSARM, MG1, Vol. 181, No. 59.

16 Ibid. Vol. 181, No. 59.

17 Brian C. Cuthbertson, ed., *The Journal of the Reverend John Payzant (1749-1834)* (Hantsport, N.S.: Lancelot Press, 1981), p. 107.

18 Ibid. p. 17.

19 Ibid. p. 18.

20 James Beverley, Barry Moody, eds., *The Life and Journal of The Rev. Mr. Henry Alline* (Hantsport, N.S.: Lancelot Press, 1982), p. 33.

21 Beverley, *Life of Alline*, p. 39.

22 Cuthbertson, *The Journal*, p. 19.

23 Ibid. p. 19.

24 B.C. Cuthbertson, "Payzant, John," *Dictionary of Canadian Biography* (Toronto: University of Toronto Press, 1979), Vol. VI, p. 573.

25 Hants County, Court of Probate, estate file 2A.

26 Lunenburg County Deeds, NSARM, RG47, Vol. 2, p. 493 (mfm).

27 1770 Census, Falmouth Township, NSARM, RG1, Vol. 443, No. 11.

28 Payzant family papers, NSARM.

29 Lunenburg County Deeds, NSARM, RG47, Vol. 1, 369 (mfm).

30 Payzant, *Payzant Families*, p. xxviii.

31 Jack F. Layton, compiler, *The Heirs of Francis Layton* ([Innisfail, Alta.]: n.p., 1986), p.2.

32 Payzant, *Payzant Families,* 189. The author says the year was 1760, when Lewis would only have been nine. In *Township of Falmouth* (p. 349), John Duncanson suggests the marriage was in 1769, when Lewis and Grace would have been 18 and 16. Since their first child was born in 1776 (according to Duncanson), I think the marriage probably took place in 1775.

33 Payzant family papers, NSARM.

34 Duncanson, *Township of Falmouth*, p. 69.

35 Manning Genealogy, Miscellaneous Manuscripts Collection, NSARM, MG100, Vol. 185, No. 37.

36 Duncanson, *Township of Falmouth*, p. 69.

37 D.G. Bell, ed., *The Newlight Baptist Journals of James Manning and James Innis* (Hantsport, N.S.: Lancelot Press, 1984), p. 89.

38 Barry M. Moody, "Manning, Edward," *Dictionary of Canadian Biography* (Toronto: University of Toronto Press, 1985), Vol. VIII, p. 612.

39 Hants County, Court of Probate, estate file 2A.

40 Cuthbertson, *The Journal*, p. 21.

41 Payzant, *Payzant Families*, p. xxiv.

42 Caroline Payzant (1822–1899) to A.D. Payzant (1868–1945), 19 February 1894. She wrote that Lucy Payzant, daughter of Lewis Payzant, grew up in the same house with her grandmother, Marie Anne.

43 Payzant, *Payzant Families*, pp. xxviii, 31, 189, 325, 261.

EPILOGUE

1 Paul Jubert, "Louis Paisant, Religionnaire et Fugitif," *Bulletin de la Société des Antiquaries de Normandie* (Caen, France: La Société, 1961-62) Tome 56, 620-633. Also microfilmed by the Genealogical Society of the Church of Jesus Christ of Latter-Day Saints, 23 Feb. 1965.

2 Marion M. Payzant, *The Payzant and Allied Jess and Juhan Families in North America* (Wollaston, Mass.: s.n., 1970) p. xxiv.

3 Club Geographique Condé-Aunay-Vassy de La Chambre du Commerce et de L'Industrie de Caen, avec le concours de la Mairie de Condé-sur-Noireau, *Condé-sur-Noireau, Savoir-Faire, Savoir-Vivre* (Condé-sur-Noireau, France: s.n., 1996?) pamphlets.

4 Abbé Louis Huet, *Histoire de Condé-sur-Noireau: Ses Seigneurs, Son Industrie, etc.* (Caen: F. Le Blanc-Hardel, 1883). Also microfilmed by the Genealogical Society of the Church of Jesus Christ of Latter-Day Saints, 1964. Original drawing at the Bibliothèque Nationale in Paris.

5 David Hey, ed., *Oxford Companion to Local and Family History* (Oxford: Oxford University Press, 1996) p. 202.

6 "Foreign Protestants" card index, NSARM, Winthrop Bell papers, MG1, Vol. 122.

7 Ibid.

8 Linda G. Wood, "The Lunenburg Indian Raids of 1756 and 1758: A New Documentary Source," *Nova Scotia Historical Review* (Halifax, N.S.: Public Archives of Nova Scotia, 1993) Vol. 13, No. 1, p. 93.

9 Howard Morley Jess to Linda G. Wood, 1 Sept. 1986.

10 Marion M. Payzant, *A Scrapbook with Notes on the Payzant and Allied Jess and Juhan Families in North America* ([Wollaston, Mass.]: s.n., 1961-63) Vol. III, p. 175.

11 James A. Wentzell (Town Clerk, Town of Lunenburg) to Linda G. Wood 25 June 1986.

12 Chris Wood, "Selling a Secure Retreat," *Macleans* (Toronto: Maclean-Hunter, 21 July 1986) p. 34.

13 Helen Creighton, *Folklore of Lunenburg County, Nova Scotia* (Toronto: McGraw-Hill Ryerson Ltd., 1950) p. 146.

14 Candace Stevenson (Director, Nova Scotia Museum Complex) to Linda G. Wood, 26 Nov. 1987.

15 Edwin C. Guillet, *The Story of Canadian Roads* (Toronto: University of Toronto Press, 1966) p. 35.

16 Stuart Trueman, *An Intimate History of New Brunswick* (Toronto: McClelland &

Stewart, 1970).

17 Payzant family papers, NSARM, MG1, Vol. 747, No.42. Lucilla Payzant, "Troublesome Times," *Montreal Witness*, circa 1880s, in notebook of Dr. Elias Nichols Payzant.

18 Payzant, *Payzant Families*, p. 44.

19 Caroline Payzant (1822-1899) to A.D. Payzant (1868-1945), 19 Feb. 1894.

20 Payzant, *A Scrapbook*, Vol. II, 41A, 41B. Lucilla Payzant to Messrs. John Dougall & Sons, 10 Oct. 1890.

21 Payzant, *Payzant Families*, p. 190.

22 *Avon Valley Golf & Country Club*, <www.nsga.ns.ca/AVON/AV.HTM> April, 2002.

23 John V. Duncanson to Linda G. Wood, 11 Oct. 1986.

24 Payzant, *A Scrapbook*, Vol. IV.

25 Payzant, *Payzant Families*, p. 190.

Image Sources

Archives de l'Archidiocèse de Québec: page 75 (66 CD, Vol A:74)

Bibliothèque municipale de Caen, France: page 7 (FNE 220)

Cliché Bibliothèque nationale de France, Paris: page 99

Corbet, Francis. *The Parish Church of Saint Helier, Jersey.* 1993: page 31

Hants County Registry of Deeds, Windsor, N.S.: page 93 (Estate File 2A)

Huet, L'Abbé Louis. *Histoire de Condé-sur-Noireau.* 1883. Archives departementales du Calvados, Caen, France: page 27

Layton, Linda: pages vi, ix, x, xv, 4, 10, 11, 29, 43, 58, 59, 81, 86, 97, 100, 101, 102, 104, 105, 107, 110, 115, 116, 117

National Archives of Canada: pages 60 (C-002708), 68 (C-000355), 71 (C-000358), 73 (C-000352), 78 (C-000354)

Payzant, Joan: page 109

Bibliography

ARCHIVAL SOURCES

1. Archives de l'Archidiocese de Québec
    Abjuration de Anne Noget, 8 décembre 1756, Registre des Abjurations, AAQ, 66CD, Vol. A:74.

2. Archives nationales du Québec, Saint-Foy, Québec
    Baptême de Louise Catherine Paisant, 27 décembre 1756,
    Registre de l'état civil de Notre-Dame-de-Québec, CN301,
    S1/36, ANQ, p. 91, verso.

3. Jersey Archive, St. Helier, Jersey, British Channel Islands
    Paroisse de St. Helier, Registre des Mariages et Enterrements, 1719–1750, Marriage of Louis Paysant to Anne Noget, p. 48, and Burial of Marie and Anne Paisant, p. 220, reference G/C/03/A1/4.

4. Archives départementales du Calvados, Caen, France, 1 B 2.199, Dossier Paysant
    Louis Paysant to De Vastan, 20 March 1738.
    Louis Paysant to De Launay, 19 September 1739.
    Louis Paysant to Pierre Lieux, 19 September 1739.
    Louis Paysant to Gosset, 19 September 1739.
    Le Courtois, Prosecution Address, December 1739.
    Le Senecal, Summons, 12 December 1739.
    Pierre Jacques Guerard, Request to Le Courtois, August 1741.
    Dumorestier, Sale of Louis Paysant's Estate, December 1741.

5. Nova Scotia Archives and Records Management, Halifax
    Shipping Returns 1753-1757, C.O. 221, Vol. 28, 228, 236, 255 (mfm).
    William Cotterell to John Pownal, 30 July 1753, RG1, Vol. 38A, p. 87.
    Journal and Letters of Col. Charles Lawrence (Halifax, 1953) (also F90 N85 AR2b).
    "Foreign Protestants" card index, Winthrop Bell papers, MG1, Vol. 122.
    Dettlieb C. Jessen's report on Lunenburg Indian attacks, 1756-1758, Miscellaneous Manuscripts Collection, MG100, Vol. 263, No. 1.
    Nova Scotia Council, minutes of meetings, 1753–1757, RG1, Vol. 210.

Churches—Lunenburg—St. Johns, Book 1, burials 1752–1787 (mfm).

Licence to Mary Paysant to Dispose of Lands, 18 August 1761, RG1, Vol. 165, No. 175.

Grantee Mary Payzant, 170 Acres, Mahone Bay, 30 August 1761, Crown Land Grants, Old Book 4, 114 (mfm).

Marriage of Caigin to Marie Anne Payzant, Falmouth Township Book 1748–1825, MG4, Vol. 31B (mfm).

Philip Payzant to Robert Melven, 22 June 1768, Lunenburg County Deeds, RG47, Vol. 2, p. 493 (mfm).

Chipman family papers, MG1, Vol. 181.

1770 Census, Falmouth Township, RG1, Vol. 443, No. 11.

Philip Paysant to Reformed Congregation, 8 January 1772, Lunenburg County Deeds, RG47, Vol. 1, p. 369 (mfm).

List of Islands in Mahone Bay 1775, Lunenburg County Land Grants, RG20, "C," Vol. 90A, doc. 22.

Manning Genealogy, Miscellaneous Manuscripts Collection, MG100, vol. 185, No. 37.

John Payzant to Adam Heckman, 7 May 1804, Lunenburg County Deeds, Vol. 10, No. 48, p. 33 (mfm).

Payzant family papers, MG1, Vol. 747, No. 42.

6. Bibliothèque protestante, Paris

Galland, A, *Histoire du protestantisme á Caen et en Basse-Normandie*, (N.P.: n.p., 1898) B.S.H.P.F., No. 2924.

Galland, A., *Le Protestantisme á Condé-sur-Noireau* (N.P.: n.p., 1900?).

LeBoitteux, A., *Les Huguenots des Isles—Histoire de l'Église Réformée de Condé-sur-Noireau, 1555–1685* (N.P.:n.p., 1906) B.S.H.P.F., No. 14584.

7. National Archives of Canada, Ottawa

Lettre de Vaudreuil au Ministre, Montréal, le 6 aôut, 1756, *Public Archives of Canada Report for 1905*, Vol. II, App. A, Part III.

8. Hants County, Windsor, Nova Scotia

Court of Probate, estate file 2A for Mary Anne Caigin.

9. Public Record Office, London, England

Louis Payzant, from Jersey to [James Payzant] concerning private matters, 25 October 1742, State Papers 36/59, pt. 2, folio 168

INTERNET SITES

Canadian Museum of Civilization Corporation, *Museum of New France, Schools in New France*, 2002. <www.civilization. ca/vmnf/education/eco00_e.html>.

Gaskell, Elizabeth, *Traits and Stories of the Huguenots, 1997.* <www.lang.nagoya-u.ac.jp/~matsuoka/EG-Traits.html>. (Written in 1853.)

Cutting to the Chase of a Long-time Debate. <www.mze.com/ sunshineparty/scalping.html>.

Huguenot Society of South Africa, *The Méreau.* <www.geocities.com/Heartland/Valley/8140/mer-e.htm>.

Scottish Field Archery Association, *Scalping: a Brief History.* <www.sfaa-archery.com/Articles/Scalping/scalping.html>.

PUBLISHED WORKS

Adams, Blaine. *The Construction and Occupation of the Barracks of the King's Bastion at Louisbourg.* Ottawa: Parks Canada, 1978.

Asselin, Jean-Pierre. "Récher, Jean-Félix." *Dictionary of Canadian Biography,* Vol. III. Toronto: University of Toronto Press, 1974.

Baird, Charles W. *History of the Huguenot Emigration to America,* Vol. II. Baltimore: Genealogical Publishing, 1973. [orig. pub. 1885].

Balleine's *History of Jersey,* rev. ed. Chichester, West Sussex: Phillimore, 1998.

Barkhouse, Joyce. "Massacre at Mahone Bay." *Canadian Frontier,* Vol. 3, No. 2. Langley, B.C.: Garnet Publishing, 1974.

Beck, J. Murray. "Cornwallis, Edward." *Dictionary of Canadian Biography,* Vol. IV. Toronto: University of Toronto Press, 1979.

Bédard, Marc André. *Les Protestants en Nouvelle-France.* Québec: La Société Historique de Québec, 1978.

Bell, D. G., ed. *The Newlight Baptist Journals of James Manning and James Innis.* Hantsport, N.S.: Lancelot Press, 1984.

Bell, Winthrop Pickard. *The "Foreign Protestants" and the Settlement of Nova Scotia,* 2nd ed. Sackville, N.B.: Mount Allison University, 1990.

Beverley, James, Barry Moody, eds. *The Life and Journal of The Rev. Mr. Henry Alline.* Hantsport, N.S.: Lancelot Press, 1982.

Bosher, J.F. *Men and Ships in the Canada Trade, 1660-1760: A Biographical Dictionary.* Ottawa: National Historic Sites, Environment Canada, 1992.

Bumsted, J.M. "Alline, Henry." *Dictionary of Canadian Biography,* Vol. IV. Toronto: University of Toronto Press, 1979.

Cautru, Camille. *L'Histoire de Condé-sur-Noireau.* Condé-sur-Noireau: Corlet, 196?.

Clio Collective. *Quebec Women: A History.* Toronto: Women's Press, 1987.

Club Geographique Condé-Aunay-Vassy de La Chambre du Commerce et de L'Industrie de Caen, avec le concours de la Mairie de Condé-sur-Noireau. *Condé-sur-Noireau, Savoir-Faire, Savoir-Vivre.* Condé-sur-Noireau, France: n.p. 1996?.

Coleman, Emma Lewis. *New England Captives Carried to Canada Between 1677 and 1760 During the French and Indian Wars.* Portland, Maine: Southworth Press, 1925.

Corbet, Francis. *The Parish Church of Saint Helier, Jersey.* St. Helier, Jersey: s.n., 1993.

Creighton, Helen. *Folklore of Lunenburg County, Nova Scotia.* Toronto: McGraw-Hill Ryerson, 1950.

Cuthbertson, B.C. "Payzant, John." *Dictionary of Canadian Biography,* Vol. VI. Toronto: University of Toronto Press, 1979.

Cuthbertson, Brian. *Lunenburg, an Illustrated History.* Halifax: Formac, 1996.

Cuthbertson, Brian C., ed. *The Journal of the Reverend John Payzant (1749–1834).* Hantsport, N.S.: Lancelot Press, 1981.

Demos, John. *The Unredeemed Captive: a Family Story from Early America.* New York: Knopf, 1994.

DesBrisay, Mather Byles. *History of the County of Lunenburg.* Belleville, Ont.: Mika Publishing, 1972. [Written in 1870.]

Donaldson, Gordon. *Battle for a Continent, Quebec 1759*. Toronto: Doubleday, 1973.

Ducros, Louis. *French Society in the Eighteenth Century*. London: G. Bell & Sons, 1926.

Duncanson, John V. *Township of Falmouth, Nova Scotia*. Belleville, Ont.: Mika Publishing, 1983.

Durant, Will and Ariel. *The Age of Voltaire*. New York: Simon & Schuster, 1965.

Eccles, W.J. "Seven Years' War." *The Canadian Encyclopedia*, Edmonton: Hurtig Publishers, 1985.

Erickson, Vincent O. "Maliseet." *Encyclopedia of World Cultures, Vol. I, North America*. Boston: G.K. Hall, 1991.

Finn, Gérard. "Le Loutre, Jean-Louis." *Dictionary of Canadian Biography*, Vol IV. Toronto: University of Toronto Press, 1979.

First Canadian Library: the Library of the Jesuit College of New France, 1632-1800. Ottawa: National Library of Canada, 1972.

Frégault, Guy. *Canada: The War of the Conquest*. Toronto: Oxford University Press, 1969.

Geographic Board of Canada. *Handbook of Indians of Canada*. Toronto: Coles, 1971. [Written in 1913.]

Gesner, Abraham. *New Brunswick*. London: Simmonds & Ward, 1847.

Gillmor, Don, Pierre Turgeon. *Canada: A People's History, Volume One*. Toronto: McClelland & Stewart, 2000.

Guillet, Edwin C. *The Story of Canadian Roads*. Toronto: University of Toronto Press, 1966.

Hey, David, ed. *Oxford Companion to Local and Family History*. Oxford: Oxford University Press, 1996.

Huet, Abbé Louis. *Histoire de Condé-sur-Noireau: Ses Seigneurs, Son Industrie, etc.* Caen: F. Le Blanc-Hardel, 1883.

J.C.B., *Travels in New France*, Sylvester K. Stevens et al., eds. Harrisburg: The Pennsylvania Historical Commission, 1941.

Johnson, Micheline D. "Germain, Charles." *Dictionary of Canadian Biography*, Vol. IV. Toronto: University of Toronto Press, 1979.

Jubert, Paul. "Louis Paisant, Religionnaire et Fugitif." *Bulletin de la Société des Antiquaries de Normandie*, Tome 56. Caen, France: La Société, 1961-62.

Kallen, Stuart A., ed. *The 1700s: Headlines in History*. San Diego, Calif.: Greenhaven Press, 2001.

Kelly, Gerald M. "Wheelwright, Esther (rebaptized Marie-Joseph), dite de l'Enfant-Jésus." *Dictionary of Canadian Biography*, Vol. IV. Toronto: University of Toronto Press, 1979.

Lacoursière, Jacques, Jean Provencher, Denis Vaugeois. *Canada-Québec: Synthèse Historique 1534–2000*. Sillery, Qué.: Septentrion, 2000.

LaPierre, Laurier L. *1759, The Battle for Canada*. Toronto: McClelland & Stewart, 1990.

Lapointe, Gabrielle. "Migeon de Branssat (Bransac), Marie-Anne, dite de la Nativité." *Dictionary of Canadian Biography*, Vol. IV. Toronto: University of Toronto Press, 1979.

Lavalée, Jean-Guy. "Dubreil de Pontbriand, Henri-Marie." *Dictionary of Canadian*

Biography, Vol. III. Toronto: University of Toronto Press, 1974.

Layton, Jack F., compiler. *The Heirs of Francis Layton*. Innisfail, Alta.: n.p., 1986.

LeBlanc, Phyllis E. "Deschamps de Boishébert et de Raffetot, Charles." *Dictionary of Canadian Biography*, Vol. IV. Toronto: University of Toronto Press, 1979.

MacMechan, Archibald. "The Payzant Captivity." *The Sunday Leader*. Halifax, N.S.: n.p., 20 February 1921.

McCreath, Peter L. & John G. Leefe. *A History of Early Nova Scotia*. Tantallon, N.S.: Four East Publications, 1982.

Moody, Barry M. "Manning, Edward." *Dictionary of Canadian Biography*, Vol. VIII. Toronto: University of Toronto Press, 1985.

Nicolle, Edmund Toulmin. *The Town of St. Helier, its Rise and Development*. Jersey, Channel Isles: Bigwood, 1931.

Palmer, R.R. *A History of the Modern World*. New York: Alfred A. Knopf, 1964.

Pargellis, Stanley. *Military Affairs in North America, 1748–1765*. Hamden Conn.: Archon Books, 1969.

Payzant, Marion M. *The Payzant and Allied Jess and Juhan Families in North America*. Wollaston, Mass.: n.p., 1970.

Payzant, Marion M. *A Scrapbook with Notes on the Payzant and Allied Jess and Juhan Families in North America*. Wollaston, Mass.: n.p., 1961–1963.

Pope, William. *Portrait of Windsor*. Windsor, N.S.: Lancelot Press, 1974.

Public Archives of Nova Scotia. "Lunenburg, Lunenburg County." *Place-Names and Places of Nova Scotia*. Belleville, Ont.: Mika Publishing, 1982.

Quiet Conquest: *The Huguenots 1685-1985*. London: Museum of London, 1985.

Rand, Silas Tertius. "Early Provincial Settlers." *The Provincial*, Vol. 1, No. 8. Halifax, N.S.: n.p., August 1852.

Reaman, G. Elmore. *The Trail of the Huguenots in Europe, the United States, South Africa and Canada*. Toronto: Thomas Allen, 1963.

Reid, J.H. Stewart, Kenneth McNaught, Harry S. Crowe, eds. *A Source-book of Canadian History: Selected Documents and Personal Papers*. Toronto: Longmans, 1964.

Rothrock, G.A. *The Huguenots: A Biography of a Minority*. Chicago: Nelson-Hall, 1979.

Silvy, Father Antoine, S.J. *Letters from North America*. Belleville, Ont.: Mika Publishing, 1980. [Written in 1709.]

Smallwood, Joseph R., ed. in chief. "Channel Islands." "Fisheries." *Encyclopedia of Newfoundland and Labrador*, Vol. 1, pp. 130, 400. N.p.: Newfoundland Book Publishers (1967) Ltd., 1981.

Smiles, Samuel. *The Huguenots: Their Settlements, Churches and Industries in England and Ireland*. London: John Murray, 1905.

Stanley, George F.G. *New France, the Last Phase 1744–1760*. Toronto: McClelland & Stewart, 1968.

Tanguay, L'Abbé Cyprien. *Dictionnaire Généalogique des Familles Canadiennes*. Montréal: Éditions Elysée, 1975. [Written in 1889].

Têtu, Henri, "M. Jean-Félix Récher, Curé de Québec, et Son Journal 1757–1760," *Bulletin des Recherches Historiques*. Québec: n.p., 1903.

Trueman, Stuart. *An Intimate History of New Brunswick.* Toronto: McClelland & Stewart, 1970.

Vachon, André. *Taking Root: Canada from 1700 to 1760.* Ottawa: Public Archives of Canada, 1985.

Waite, P.B., ed. *Pre-Confederation,* Vol. 2. Scarborough, Ont.: Prentice-Hall, 1965.

Webster, J. Clarence, ed. *Memorial on Behalf of the Sieur de Boishébert.* Saint John, N.B.: New Brunswick Museum, 1942. [Written in 1763.]

Witherspoon, John. "Journal of John Witherspoon," *Collections of the Nova Scotia Historical Society 1878-1884,* Vol. II. Belleville, Ont.: Mika Publishing, 1976. [Written 1757–1759.]

Wood, Chris. "Selling a Secure Retreat." *Macleans.* Toronto: Maclean-Hunter, 21 July 1986.

Wood, Linda G. "The Lunenburg Indian Raids of 1756 and 1758: A New Documentary Source." *Nova Scotia Historical Review,* Vol. 13, No. 1. Halifax, N.S.: Public Archives of Nova Scotia, 1993.

Wood, Linda G. "Murder Among the Planters: A Profile of Malachi Caigin of Falmouth, Nova Scotia." *Nova Scotia Historical Review,* Vol. 16, No. 1. Halifax N.S.: Public Archives of Nova Scotia, 1996.

Wright, Esther Clark. *The Saint John River and its Tributaries.* Wolfville, N.S.: n.p., 1966.